LIVE SMALL
LIVE MODERN
THE BEST OF BEAMS AT HOME

First English edition published in the United States of America by Rizzoli International Publications, Inc.
300 Park Avenue South, New York, NY 10010 www.rizzoliusa.com

Live Small / Live Modern: The Best of Beams at Home

For BEAMS Co., Ltd. and Takarajimasha, Inc.
Editors: Shuichi Fujisada, Tomomi Sakurai,
and Sachiho Nomoto
Additional Editors: Yukari Ohyama, Yusuke Osawa,
Erina Watanabe, Izumi Kaji, Sachie Minamoto, Risako
Hayashi, Kaito Yoshikawa, Mitsugu Sudo,
and Ayako Ikegame (RCKT/Rocket Company*)
Photographs: Shin Hamada, Tomoya Uehara, Miho Noro,
Amazon Kajiyama, Kazuki Watanabe, Takeshi Abe,
Ittetsu Matsuoka, Suguru Kumaki, Taro Hirano, Ai Ezaki,
Kanako Hamada, Miki Yamauchi, Risa Kato,
Ayumi Yamamoto, Shigeki Orita, Kazuhiro Tsushima
(TONETONE PHOTOGRAPH), and Yuki Kinoshita
Illustration: Kahoko Sodeyama
Writers: Mayumi Abe, Megumi Yamashita, Aya Miyauchi,
Azumi Hasegawa, Tomoko Minooka, Takatoshi Takebe
(THISIS(NOT)MAGAZINE/LIVERARY), Mari Horio,
and Shiori Fujii
Art Direction: Noriteru Minezaki ((STUDIO))
Design: Kosuke Shono ((STUDIO))
DTP: Itaru Mizutani and Keiko Miyoshi
Production: Hiroshi Doiji, Toshihiro Yasutake,
Manabu Chigira, Aki Uchiyama, and Aya Satake
Editorial Coordination: Kiyotaka Yaguchi and Noriko Aoki
Project Coordination: Takahiko Sato

For Rizzoli International Publications
Editor: Ian Luna
Project Editor: Meaghan McGovern
Production: Kaija Markoe & Olivia Russin
Translation: Marie Iida
Design Coordination: Eugene Lee

Publisher: Charles Miers

Rizzoli wishes to thank the participation of the following
individuals:
Shuichi Fujisada and Mariko Hasegawa at Takarajimasha, Inc.;
everyone at Japan Uni Agency

Printed in China

2018 2019 2020 2021 2022 / 10 9 8 7 6 5 4 3 2 1
Library of Congress Control Number: 2018967229
ISBN: 978-0-8478-6525-3

LIVE SMALL LIVE MODERN
THE BEST OF BEAMS AT HOME

RIZZOLI
NEW YORK

INTRODUCTION

I.

Things that you do at home: You wake up in the morning and grind coffee beans, letting them bloom with piping hot water. While you nibble on a piece of toast, you tend to your ferns and cacti with just the right amount of water. You make conversation with your family, or your roommate. You take a quick shower, and don the outfit you've chosen for the day. In the afternoon, the laundry strung across the balcony flutters in the wind as it dries. In the empty house, your cat seeks out a sunny spot and curls up into a ball. The sunlight shifts little by little throughout the day. In the evening, when you come home, you look up and see your house lit up warmly from within. Maybe your kids come running to greet you by the door. I'm home, you say. Welcome home, you hear. Tonight, you and yours are sharing a hotpot with lettuce and pork. Afterwards, you reflect on your plans for the weekend, perhaps a brunch with friends, a leisurely walk through the park with your dog, binging on a favorite TV series, or a camping trip in the country. When the night deepens, you take a hot bath, and fall asleep, safe and sound.

The place where we spend the most of our time is the place that gives us the fullest sense of belonging. The meaning of home is a diverse as its occupants and is therefore the site of as many unique stories. There is no correct shape or form to a home.

II.

Since its founding in Harajuku, Tokyo in 1976, BEAMS has remained at the vanguard of lifestyle retailing in Japan. Conceived as a tiny, 231-square-foot "American lifestyle shop," offering everything from t-shirts to mousetraps, BEAMS pioneered the "select shop concept" and has since developed into a global brand with more than 150 shops across Japan, East Asia and Southeast Asia. A major lifestyle retailer with businesses in fashion, home furnishing, arts, café culture and dining, BEAMS' reach and influence extends to tastemakers in Western Europe and North America.

BEAMS' desire to become a comprehensive lifestyle brand has expanded geographically as well as notionally since its inception, and is more convinced than ever in the power of things.

Even as we as a society has moved on from an era in which happiness was equivalent to owning a large quantity of things, to a time when we can access limitless information online, there is a simple joy in being surrounded by objects we like. From toys given to us as children, to handmade tableware, and our favorite pieces of clothing, these items remind us of their makers, and help us imagine a way of life.

III.

Well-loved things, accompanied with its own distinct histories, are imbued with an affirming power. And the skill of selecting and combining things sourced from different cultures—Japanese *mingei* folk craft, mid-century Scandinavian furniture, Chemex coffeemakers, African art, American industrial lampshades, for example—is what creates the unique rhythm, the comfortable clutter to our busy, 21st-century lives.

This ability to order and reorder these things is what generates a sense of comfort, one that is common to the over sixty homes featured in this book. Inhabited by professionals that are either in the direct employ of BEAMS, or else vocationally associated with the brand, the lives led by these individuals and their families open a window into modern urban life. The things they have elected to surround themselves populate a range of living situations, from detached homes at the edges of town, to impossibly tiny apartments in the heart of the metropolis. Taken together or individually, the homes in this book (selected too, from volumes 1, 2 and 3 of *BEAMS at Home*) teach us a way to connect—with style—to the things we love the most.

IV.

What are some of the secrets we can glean from the lifestyles of BEAMS staff in order to create a place of safety and comfort? The first step is to deepen your knowledge of the things you love. It could be Star Wars memorabilia, bicycles, pottery, music, and of course, clothes. The second step is to keep only the things that you love. Native American culture teaches us that even among stones that look alike, we can chose the one that fits us perfectly. The third step is to interact with the things you love everyday and do so in an environment that feels comfortable. And finally, the fourth step is to connect to the power inherent in the things you love and let that sense of connection expand from your room to the town and city you live in.

The things we love connect us to new people and their stories. That is how a *home*town is created. BEAMS has set out into the world to present these ideas in *Live Small / Live Modern*, firm in the belief that with a little inspiration, we all can come back to a place called home at the close of every day.

— BEAMS and Ian Luna

TABLE OF CONTENTS

008

Yusuke Yamashita
Kobe, Hyogo

The living room wall is decorated with a Kilim tapestry, to which Yamashita added his own arrangement with driftwood. The formal beauty of the rubber tree acquires a dash of playfulness with the Kay Bojesen monkey. A quick look through Yamashita's books reveal his interest in surfing.

Yamashita's home is as bright and refreshing as the brilliant sunshine pouring into the room. "We know what we want." True to his words, Yamashita's large living room teems with high-quality Scandinavian furniture and Japanese ceramics. Thriving plants are also arranged tastefully around the room. As the couple sit down to relax on their favorite sofa, they seem to emit their own light of happiness.

What is the most important theme of your lifestyle?
A life with plenty of sunshine and greeneries.

What is the most important way to spend your time?
Spending time with my wife. We particularly enjoy sharing a meal.

What is the theme or rule for your home?
Instead of things that are brand new, I like things with character. So, I try to look for vintage pieces as much as possible.

What is the most cherished item in your home?
Hans J. Wegner sofa.

Do you have a favorite interior design brand or store?
Swanky Systems in Osaka.

Do you have any advice for people who have trouble keeping a tidy home?
Declutter!

What kind of fashion style do you like?
I'm in charge of women's fashion, so I'm always conscious of styles that are simple and pretty.

Which item of clothing do you find most useful when coordinating your everyday style?
A blue shirt. Shirts are the foundation of many of my ensembles, so they are important.

What's the best thing about working for BEAMS?
Being blessed with amazing colleagues.

What was the most memorable episode you've had at work?
There are so many of them, but I cherish my encounters with people.

012

1

3

2

4

1. A wedding board, ordered from BEAMS, sits atop the George Nelson bench.

2. A set of Maison Margiela matryoshka dolls. A bare, mysterious objet d'art, it is made of smooth, white lacquered wood with no design.

3. Yamashita and his wife also love ceramics. An attractive collection including pottery from Okinawa, Onta ware, and pieces from Shussai Gama kiln.

4. A stand by Frank Lloyd Wright accents the room.

The various greeneries scattered around the room have a gentle effect.

5. On their days off, the couple heads into the kitchen. The loving couple's favorite pastime is to cook and share a meal.

6. The Japanese-style room boasts a multinational array of interior décors including a low table by Eames, a chair from Okinawa, and a Hans J. Wegner poster. They look right at home on the Ryukyu tatami.

014

"The fact that I can ride my bike to the sea made me want to live here," Tozawa explains by way of introducing her passion for surfing. Her room is filled with Native American motifs, surfboards, and skateboards—all things indispensable to her lifestyle. She likes to get up early in the morning and carry her surfboard out to sea. There, she gets to experience nature with her whole body, feeling the ocean breeze and the waves. The freedom to enjoy who she is without pretense may be the ultimate definition of luxury.

What's your hobby?
Surfing and going on walks.

Do you have any collections or things you can't resist buying?
Lately I'm partial to swimsuits. I always buy snow globes whenever I travel.

What's your storage rule?
I can't really say since I'm not good at storing, but I try to put things that I like where I can see them.

What is the most important theme of your lifestyle?
To live close to the sea.

What is the most cherished item in your home?
The blue chair a friend and I painted together in my previous home.

Do you have a favorite interior design brand or store?
Mar-Vista Garden in Chigasaki.

Which item of clothing do you find most useful when coordinating your everyday style?
Vans sneakers, a pack of Hanes T-shirts, denim.

What is your source of information for interior design and fashion?
Anna Magazine.

What do you hope to purchase next?
I'd love to buy a new surfboard. And a pair of jeans.

What's the best thing about working for BEAMS?
Meeting many people I would like to know forever! Having had the chance to start surfing!

What was the most memorable episode you've had at work?
When my boss took me to America.

A denim bag hanging from a wall is emblazoned with pins and badges inspired by Tozawa's love of street culture. "I built a skateboard when I traveled to the U.S. three years ago. I didn't have a bag to carry it home, so I looked for a stylish bag and found this one."

016

1. "A pair of jeans is like a uniform to me," says Tozawa. The vintage Levi's 701XX is a recent purchase that she loves.
2. Rings and bracelets are kept together in ceramic catch all bowls. Instead of tucking them away, they are displayed as part of the interior décor.
3. A colorful array of beloved Vans sneakers. "They feel so comfortable. I choose them in the same way I choose underwear."
4. A selection of favorite accessories hangs on the wall. "I don't know if it's because my parents loved America so much, but ever since I was little I have admired Native American culture," Tozawa explains. Beads, feathers, and other

light and natural materials complement her room perfectly.
5. Maps purchased at Tozawa's past travel destinations bear the mark of places she has visited. She keeps the maps on the wall as inspiration for her future travels.
6. Polaroid photos taken during a trip to New York last year. Memories—the scenes she saw and the expressions of her friends—are always the best interior decoration.
7. Snow globes of varying sizes accumulate in one corner of the room. "I always buy them as a personal souvenir whenever I travel. Most of them are from America, though. It's fun to look at because each area offers a different design."

020

Masato Honma
Kashiwa, Chiba

A gentle breeze flows through the house built next to a small Japanese shrine. Honma's residence occupies the second floor of the house he built with his parents two autumns ago and on weekends friends gather in his sunny living room. Sitting around a table lined with his wife's professional-level cooking, friends and family talk about their life, work and their shared hobby, surfing. "It's amazing how happy I feel when I'm home," Honma says, laughing shyly. His bright smile tells us all we need to know about his living space.

What is the most important theme of your lifestyle?
To live where you can feel the sea. Comfort.

Why did you choose to live in this area?
It's close to both the city and nature. It's easy to get out to the sea.

How do you alleviate stress?
Surfing!

What is the theme or rule for your home?
It should evoke the sea.

What is the most cherished item in your home?
My surfboards. I have four. My current favorite is the board by Milne.

Do you have a favorite interior design brand or store?
Issui Pottery.

Do you have any advice for people who have trouble keeping a tidy home?
I can't stay tidy either. I recommend living with someone who can.

What kind of fashion style do you like?
Something with a sense of humor. Anything that makes me look thinner.

Which fashion brands do you prefer when creating your own sense of style?
BEAMS. I like both their original and selected brands. There are so many interesting items.

What is your source of information for interior design and fashion?
Nakisurf, which is maintained by the pro surfer and photographer Mitsuhide Funaki.

What do you hope to purchase next?
I'd like a surfboard, but my wife says I can't because I just recently bought one.

022

Honma had requested that the multicolored tiles in the kitchen be vertical, but they ended up horizontal. "Oh well, they're not so bad," says Honma, easygoing as usual. The Channel Islands surf board placed in the corner of the living room brings in the sea breeze. Honma's bookcase showcases his love for BEAMS.

024

1. A tiny cactus in a corner of the kitchen serves as a gentle reminder to take it easy.

2. On the bookshelf: A poster of Honma's beloved Nakisurf; building blocks by Landscape Products and a touch of green; a figurine of a fish which Honma's wife fell in love with in Bali.

3. & 4. Honma's wife slices freshly made roast beef. The talented chef is a whiz at multitasking.

5. A wooden tray holds everyday accessories and jewelry.

6. The east-facing room, currently used for storage, will become the child's room in the future.

7. The family's bedroom adjacent to the living room has a simple and modern air.

8. One of Honma's greatest pleasures in life is his wife's cooking. Roast beef with mushroom and chicken gizzard ajillo, fried firefly squid and deep-water shrimp, and seared skipjack tuna seasoned with gochujang. Edo Kiriko, Ryukyu glassware from Okinawa, and plates from Issui Pottery are an excellent companion to the delicious meal.

Yutaka Eguchi
Hiroshima City, Hiroshima

The interior of Eguchi's home takes its cues from cacti to all things Hawaiian, with the occasional surfer culture thrown in. Despite its location—the first floor of an apartment building—his space reminds you of the vast sea and the earth, thanks to the array of cacti, taxidermy, and small accessories that remind us of Waikiki Beach. The living room with its relaxed mood feels spacious as it continues out to the veranda. "I like to start my days off by watering my garden." That is exactly what we find Eguchi doing when we visit him, his movements that of a seasoned gardener.

What is the most important theme of your lifestyle?
To live naturally among my favorite things and plants.

What is the theme or rule for your home?
To have a theme for each wall or room and always use plants as the centerpiece.

What is the most cherished item in your home?
My cat. It's a Bengal cat with leopard spots.

Do you have any collection or things you can't resist buying?
Cacti, bandanas, sunglasses, Hawaiian goods.

Can you tell us how you started collecting all these cacti?
When I went to volunteer after the Hiroshima landslides (in 2014), I saw that cacti collectors also suffered considerable damage. They told me it has become difficult to grow cacti, so I took them in and I'm caring for them to this day.

Do you have a favorite interior design brand or store?
Shussai Gama kiln, Onta ware, and hardware stores.

What kind of fashion style do you like?
A grown-up surfer style.

Which fashion brands do you prefer when creating your own sense of style?
Remi Relief, Vans, Needles, Patagonia.

What is your source of information for interior design and fashion?
Casa Brutus, Facebook, Instagram, Flickr.

What do you hope to purchase next?
A totem pole, African folkcraft, tikis a nd other Polynesian goods.

What's the best thing about working for BEAMS?
I've gained many customers and friends.

Pictured next to Eguchi is an old skateboard deck, reused as a planter.

The baby cactus, grown from seeds, will be replanted as it grows bigger. The large cacti pictured below were inherited from a friend. "There are some that are much older than me," says Eguchi.

1. Eguchi's home overflows with greeneries both inside and out. The ukulele, which his wife started practicing about three years ago, is displayed alongside the hula doll purchased at BEAMS.

2. The name of Eguchi's beloved cat, Mahalo, means "gratitude" in Hawaiian.

3. Statuettes of Tikis, which first spread from Polynesia around a thousand years ago, are worshipped as deities in Hawaii.

4. Eguchi often dons Oakley sunglasses when he commutes to work on his bike.

5. The film poster of *Sprout*, a surfing movie by the renowned creator, surfer, and skateboarder Thomas Campbell. Beautiful photos of sunset beaches.

6. The stately dining table was purchased at a friend's interior décor shop. The chairs are Eames Shell chairs and the lighting, purchased at BEAMS, is a PH4/3 Pendant by Louis Poulsen.

7. Eguchi likes to brew coffee for his family from time to time.

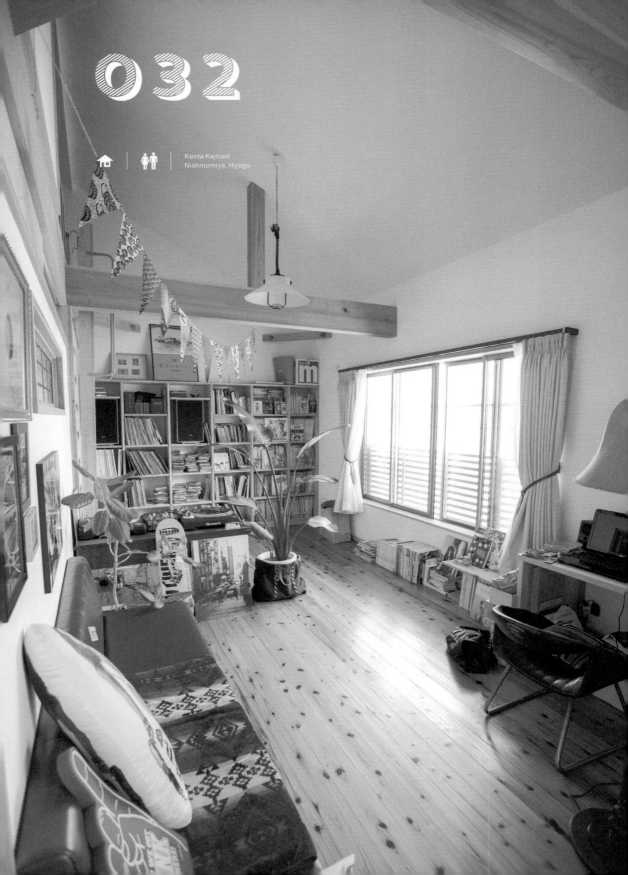

032

Kenta Kajitani
Nishinomiya, Hyogo

Newlyweds in a newly constructed home. Kajitani, who started his life together with his wife in this brand-new space, is a celebrity at BEAMS. Together with his wife, a former BEAMS staffer, they worked as visual models for BEAMS' advertisements and were featured together in numerous posters and promotional materials. "The environment around us is the natural result of us living with the things we like," Kajitani says of their home, where the couple's beloved items gather to create a comfortable space.

What is the most important theme of your lifestyle?
I like to live with natural things as much as possible.

What is your theme or rule for interior design?
We don't let our tastes become too fixed. We just place the things we each like however way we like.

What is the most cherished item in your home?
A stool by Artek, given to us by a colleague as a wedding gift.

Do you have any collection or things you can't resist buying?
Records and T-shirts with designs that appealed to me.

Do you have a favorite interior design brand or store?
Shark Attack in Osaka.

Do you have any advice for people who have trouble keeping a tidy home?
Make your home look good even when it's cluttered. Make it look nice and lived in.

What kind of fashion style do you like?
I respect black culture, so I like hip-hop and street styles.

Which fashion brands do you prefer when creating your own sense of style?
Salvatore Piccolo; Stile Latino; BBP.

Are there any magazines, books, or people that inspire your interior design and fashion?
Warp, *Leon*, and *Men's EX*. Mostly fashion magazines. Ever since I fell in love with clothes when I was in grade school, I've studied fashion with magazines.

What do you hope to purchase next?
A cupboard and a desk.

What is your personal mantra?
Fresh.

1. Kajitani's love of records finally propelled him to create a record listening booth. He spends every spare moment here savoring his records.

2. A fan of black music, Kajitani can't help but add to his record collection.

3. The bedroom door was an antique shop find. Kajitani always dreamed of living in an open, single room, but his wife insisted on separating "at least the bedroom" so he created a wall to section off the space. The stickers his wife put on the wall accent the room.

4. The sliding entrance door was also purchased at an antique shop, just like the bedroom door. The numers add a nice touch. The couple, who eschewed living inside a prefabricated mold, found it important to be able to reflect their own style through the parts and layout of their new home.

038

Terry Ellis
Keiko Kitamura
London, UK

This is the London home of Ellis and Kitamura. Built in the 19th century, the home has been carefully restored and renovated and crowded with furniture, pottery, art, and books that the couple have collected over the years from their travels around the world. Since they like to try things themselves before selling them at the store, their home is a testing ground for the kind of lifestyle suggested by BEAMS and Fennica. Various trends, from mid-century modern and Scandinavian to folkcrafts and Okinawan influences, began here.

Launched by BEAMS in 2003 to serve as a bridge between design and craft, Fennica (formerly BEAMS MODERN LIVING) presents a style that combines traditional Japanese hand-icraft with new and old designs collected from Northern Europe. Fennica's less global, more local theme is demonstrated in its lineup, encompassing an entire lifestyle, from men's and women's wear to tableware, home interiors and cuisine.

What is the most important theme of your lifestyle?
To always have an open mind. Whether it's clothes, furniture, or food, if you're curious, try and test it.

How do you like to spend your day off?
We got to the market in Brixton and purchase Jamaican avocados and eat them at home. If it's a longer holiday we like to relax in Barbados or Okinawa.

What is your theme or rule for interior design?
We try not to have a specific theme or rule; we mix things from various generations and countries with eclectic designs.

What is the most cherished item in your home?
Ellis: A custom made rocking chair from Matsumoto Mingei Kagu (available at Fennica).
Kitamura: A cabinet that was given to us by Sori Yanagi.

Do you have any collection or things you can't resist buying?
Ellis: A straw raincoat. I collect old Japanese raincoats made of straws and other materials such as seaweed.
Kitamura: Wooden toys such as kokeshi dolls (pictured here: a kokeshi designed by Kaj Franck).

Do you have a favorite interior design brand or store?
Artek in Helsinki, Svenskt Tenn in Stockholm.

Do you have any advice for people who have trouble keeping a tidy home?
When you have a storage room it's easy to keep your home tidy.

What kind of fashion style do you like?
For that you'll need to look at Fennica originals.

Are there any magazines, books, or people that inspire your interior design and fashion?
The journal *Mingei* which is published by Japan Mingei Association.

What do you hope to purchase next?
Indigo-dyed textiles from Africa.

How do you hone your sense of style?
Mix and match various things and find something that suits your sensibility through trial and error. Touch handmade crafts, not brand goods, in person. (Let Fennica be your guide!)

What is your personal mantra?
"Try it, love it, use it." (Soetsu Yanagi, philosopher and founder of the Mingei Movement, on the beauty of utility.)

040

1. Old Japanese cloaks that Ellis likes to collect adorn the walls. They are the epitome of beauty of utility. Inside the cabinets are priceless ceramics collection including the work of Noriyasu Tsuchiya, Shoji Hamada, Bernard Leach, and even those from the Song dynasty. On top of the cabinet are works by Markku Kosonen.

2. Wrapped around Kitamura's wrist is a reindeer leather bracelet made by the Swedish designer Maria Rudman. It is available at Fennica.

3. Decorating the living room wall is a kite chain with a hundred feet, a traditional folkcraft from the Takamatsu region of Kagawa prefecture. The lighting is by Josef Frank and the wall shelf is by Bruno Mathsson. Styles that span both decades and country—Japan, Scandinavia, modern, and the traditional—are mixed together.

4. A corner of the reception room. An Edmund De Waal pot, a colorful embriodery by Alighiero Boetti, and a masterpiece by the woodblock printmaker Bokunen Naka are placed on the cabinet by Robert Heritage. No matter the genre, items lining this room have all been sourced around the world with the couple's keen, curatorial eye.

Ritsumi Murata
Yokosuka, Kanagawa

The first thing that captures our eyes as we are ushered into the room is the large wall of records and acoustic equipment. "This room is something we just had to have," Murata says of the record room, a space that he and his wife, both music lovers, had dreamed of for years. Murata's residence has been reconstructed from his wife's birth home, complete with a high, custom-made ceiling and walls constructed of natural materials. When the uplifting breeze flows into the home from the sea nearby, it gets easy to lose track of the time. "We love it here and find it hard to leave." There's an enduring charm to living close to one's roots.

How do you like to spend your day off?
Doing nothing and being lazy.

What is the most important way to spend your time?
Listening to records and relaxing.

What is the theme or rule for your home?
Natural materials and colors.

What is your favorite spot in your home and how do you like to spend time there?
In front of my record shelf. I like to listen to music and play around with my musical instruments.

How many records do you own?
I've been collecting them since I was a student, so I probably have at least 2000.

Which is your go-to record shop?
Big Love in Harajuku.

Most memorable record?
The Danish band Gangway; the British bands Fairground Attraction and Orange Juice.

Most memorable live performance?
When Primal Scream performed in Japan in '91, right after they released Screamadelica.

Where do you get inspiration for your interior décor?
The picture I had in mind was a tambourine studio with an array of records and equipment, like the one used by the Swedish band The Cardigans.

Do you have any advice for people who have trouble keeping a tidy home?
Let's start by putting things away.

What kind of fashion style do you like?
I think American casual is my foundation.

Which item of clothing do you find most useful when coordinating your everyday style?
Hats.

What's the best thing about working for BEAMS?
BEAMS is a brand that I've loved for so long, that I'm grateful to be formally associated with it.

1. Murata's residence is situated close to the ocean. It's possible to feel the sea breeze in their garden.

2. The large kitchen and dining area, with its warm-colored walls, functions as the heart of the family's lives. The climate of their home base—cool in the summer and warm in the winter—adds to its appeal.

3. Murata's specialty is the guitar. The day when he can form a family band with his oldest son, here practicing the drums, may not be so far away.

4. Murata admires the mix of stylish exterior and warm interior as seen in Electric Cottage, the office of Hiroshi Fujiwara. The silver exterior wall of his home, made as close to his ideal as possible, has the added benefit of being durable.

5. Family's treasured photos as well as flyers are on display.

6. The living room, with its large dining room table and equally dynamic ceiling, feels truly liberating. The walls, made of diatomaceous earth, have the warmth that only natural materials can provide.

7. Murata used to play in a band. His collection of instruments include electric, bass, and acoustic guitars, and a drum set.

052

  Hiroshi Doiji
Kawasaki, Kanagawa

Sounds of children playing in the park across the street reverberate in the calm atmosphere. Doiji's residence located on the fifth floor of a low-rise apartment building, comes with an expansive outdoor terrace accessible from the living room and the children's room. Doiji's twin daughters, just home from elementary school, are absorbed in gossip out on the terrace. The spacious terrace, which can be used comfortably as an extension of interior, gives their life room to expand. In this home, family time flows naturally and with ease. The head of the family brews some coffee, as if to accent the rhythm of their days with a leisurely break.

What is the most important theme of your lifestyle?
It depends on how we feel each day so we don't center our lives around a particular pattern, but we do try to incorporate an environment where the children can have fun inside the home too. That's the reason we moved from the city center to the suburbs, where we can easily access parks with plenty of nature. I also like places with lots of light. Our apartment is not a high-rise building but it gets plenty of sunlight and the open, refreshing atmosphere is something we were after.

What is your theme or rule for interior design?
We don't have one in particular, but we do like to live surrounded by plants.

What is your favorite spot in your home and how do you like to spend time there?
I like to relax on the terrace. Our home is surrounded on all sides by cherry blossom trees, so come spring it's a fantastic place to take in the view while sitting on a carpet of cherry blossom petals.

What is the most cherished item in your home?
I like my PH Snowball by Louis Poulsen, antiques by PH5, and sofa by Hans J. Wegner.

Do you have any collection or things you can't resist buying?
Nothing major, but I do collect terrariums and succulents. I also purchase snow globes whenever I go abroad.

Do you have a favorite interior design brand or store?
Talo, which has a wide selection of Scandinavian furniture. I also like flea markets overseas.

Do you have any advice for people who have trouble keeping a tidy home?
It oppresses the space when there are too many things stored up high, so try to store as much as possible in low places.

Which fashion brands do you prefer when creating your own sense of style?
BEAMS.

Are there any magazines, books, or people that inspire your interior design and fashion?
Many different interior design magazines, starting with *Casa Brutus*. I also often get inspired from movies.

How do you hone your sense of style?
I think taste or sensibility comes from all of your five senses. It's something that can be nurtured by eating good food, listening to music, and looking at beautiful things.

What is your personal mantra?
Where there's a will, there's a way.

1. Poul Henningsen's masterpiece, a pendant lamp designed in 1958, illuminates the dining room wall where a collection of photos of Doiji's daughters taken by Takashi Homma are displayed. The record of their growth, marked by a new photo every year, is an irreplaceable treasure.

2. The twins don't mind sharing the single children's room. The room is laid out so that each of their desks faces the wall, allowing them to focus on their studies. Outside the window is the terrace that doubles as a playground where the girls like to ride their unicycle.

3. Plants that can also thrive indoors occupy the window-sill. This particular section, arranged around Diptyque room fragrance and candles, highlights the sophisticated taste of Doiji's wife, a designer of handbags and other fashion accessories.

4. The antique framed photo of his little daughters is another of Doiji's treasures. The drink bottle of Stumptown Coffee Roasters is a souvenir from Portland.

058

Hiroaki Konishi
Saitama City, Saitama

At the center of Konishi family's life are their beloved dogs, Nico and Milk. On sunny days off the family like to go on walks at the dog run. On days they spend at home they like to relax on the Hans J. Wegner sofa. The living room, with its coterie of vintage Scandinavian furniture, is decorated with unique plants, stuffed animals, candles, and artwork with dog motifs. Theirs is a life full of canine love.

What is the most important theme of your lifestyle?
Animals. Especially our Boston Terriers Nico (4) and Milk (2).

What is your theme or rule for interior design?
We have dogs so we don't place anything on the floor. We opt for furniture with legs.

What is the most cherished item in your home?
Our Hans J. Wegner sofa. It's a three-seater but we swapped out one of the seats to add a pop of color.

Do you have any collections or things you can't resist buying?
Items and figurines with dog motifs; camera lenses.

Do you have a favorite interior design brand or store?
The Scandinavian furniture brand Talo.

Do you have any advice for people who have trouble keeping a tidy home?
You need courage to get rid of things. Don't think of tidying as a hassle. Make tidying a habit.

What do you hope to purchase next?
A cleaning robot.

How do you hone your sense of style?
It comes with experience.

062

1. Konishi's home is populated by many objects with animal motifs. Unique cats made by Lisa Larson and Hakusan pottery hold court on top of the T.V. set. Plants purchased at the Ozaki Flower Park in Shakujiidai and Hikone, Shiga prefecture, where Konishi is from, create a beautiful ambience as they intermingle with sunlight filtering in through the Alvar Aalto curtains.

2. Stuffed animals of Nico and Milk made by Zero And Mami, a brand owned by the family's artist friend.

3. Nico and Milk's room. Their outfits are kept in a chest purchased at Fusion Interiors. "If we count the ones we keep in the apartment storage room, we probably have over 120 outfits," Konishi says. On top of the drawer are an owl-shaped moneybox, bird figurines, and a commemorative plate from the Koshien, the National High School Baseball Championship of Japan.

4. The walk-in closet, which clinched their decision to buy the home, is where the couple keeps more than a hundred pairs of shoes. "My wife is more of a fashion addict than I am!" says Konishi.

064

Jenny Gold

Kazutaka Hasegawa
Shinagawa, Tokyo

Hasegawa's home showcases a contemporary sensibility that deftly remixes unlikely things while embracing an eclectic street culture. His home has the mood of a teenager's secret hideout. "I hope my room can stand as a counterpoint to everyone else's," he says. True to his words, the adolescent-like room that weaves a medley of items together can best be described as a high-quality chaos that's truly one of a kind.

What is your theme or rule for interior design?
I like things that visitors will enjoy. I don't fixate on the country of origin or era.

What is the most cherished item in your home?
My coffee table.

Do you have any collections or things you can't resist buying?
I collect anything that moves me.

Do you have a favorite interior design brand or store?
Sign in Hiroo; Tranship in Musashikoyama; Jantiques in Nakameguro; D&Department in Kuhonbutsu.

Do you have any advice for people who have trouble keeping a tidy home?
Don't force yourself to tidy. Try to tidy in one go when the mood strikes.

What kind of fashion style do you like?
Basic and exciting.

Which fashion brands do you prefer when creating your own sense of style?
Unused; Dries Van Noten.

Are there any magazines, books, or people that inspire your interior design and fashion?
Transit; the *Mingei no Kyokasho* (Mingei Textbook) series; *Brutus*.

How do you hone your sense of style?
Hang out with people from all walks of life.

What is your personal mantra?
One chance in a lifetime.

1. Hasegawa and his wife discuss their travels. The couple, who live in a space that mixes influences from various countries, cultures, and eras, are fair, open, and playful in their eclecticism. Placed together with Eames furniture and objects are antique lamps and flower vases with religious motifs, as well as customized ivory and stickers from the '80s. We also glimpsed an autograph of Shawn Stussy.
2. The Suicoke vodka bottle is as charming as it is strangely ceremonial. The item, which Hasegawa received as a gift, is something he treasures for its street culture-inspired visual.
3. Displayed in the hallway just inside the entrance is an antique butterfly specimen. Looming above is the distinctive presence of a mountain goat. The horned rabbit, known as a Jackalope, is a mythical creature of American folklore and its replica was imported from its native land.
4. Plants and religious figurines make an odd contrast. The geometric doorstopper is a vintage find from George Nelson.

069

070

Kohei Kanie
Aya Kanie
Sumida, Tokyo

Tucked under Kanie's arm is the latest addition to his collection: a full-scale Stormtrooper helmet. Kanie's Star Wars room is not limited to action figures. Among the collection are silkscreened posters by the illustrator Yu Nagaba purchased at BEAMS T. A sweet illustration of Luke and Yoda.

Kanie's home is nestled at the foot of Tokyo Skytree, a neighborhood where stores and wooden homes from the bygone days of Tokyo still remain. Walking through Kanie's living room full of nostalgic, Japanese trinkets, we finally reach the corner dedicated to his passion. This is where Kanie gathers, arranges, dusts off, and adores his collection time and again. "One side of this shelf is dedicated to Kenner, the other to Hasbro." Star Wars items are arranged in a beautiful configuration, and the vast number of 31-inch action figures lined together makes for an impressive display. This is no kid's play—a grownup fandom is a serious business.

What's your hobby?
Collecting Star Wars action figures.

Do you have any collections or things you can't resist buying?
Star Wars merchandise; tableware.

What's your storage rule?
To surround myself with things I like.

How do you like to spend time at home?
I like to refresh by watching movies.

What is the theme or rule for your home?
To incorporate Japanese things.

Do you have a favorite interior design brand or store?
D&Department Tokyo, Cibone.

Why did you choose to live in this area?
I was attracted by the warm humanity of Tokyo's old downtown.

What kind of fashion style do you like?
A natural style that feels suited to me.

Which item of clothing do you find most useful when coordinating your everyday style?
Watches.

Which fashion brands do you prefer when creating your own sense of style?
Auralee.

What is your source of information for interior design and fashion?
Hypebeast.

How do you hone your sense of style?
Find someone who feels cool to you.

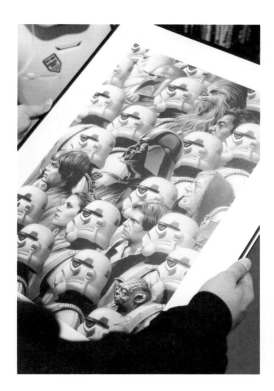

How did you begin working for BEAMS?
I've admired BEAMS ever since I was in junior high.

What's the best thing about working for BEAMS?
Getting to meet all kinds of people.

What was the most memorable episode you've had at work?
The moment when the bond I have with my customers deepens.

Captions for page 74:
1. & 2. Amplifying the Japanese mood in the living room is the indigo "rag," which was created by patching together cloth from the Taisho and Meiji era of Japan. Kanie's wife, who also works on the BEAMS JAPAN staff, saw it in the store and felt she had to have one. "I've always liked things that feel traditionally Japanese," Kanie says. There are other Japanese trinkets around the room, like the *kokeshi* doll from Fennica and the *maneki-neko* figurine. Kanie received the Karimoku dining table from an older colleague and treasures it dearly.

3. Plants are the second most ubiquitous item adorning his home. The dried flowers were purchased at logi Plants & Flowers.

4. Bottles of homemade plum wine in the kitchen. Kanie's wife has been steeping a bottle every year for a few years now.

5. Figures are sorted into shelves by maker and size. The left shelf is dedicated to Kenner and Hasbro merchandise; 12-, 6-, and 3.75-inch action figures are displayed random-ly. 31-inch figures by JAKKS PACIFIC are grouped together on the right shelf.

6. Kanie likes to unwind on the sofa and watch movies. A STAR WARS series is a given.

7. Stormtrooper action figures released in 1996. When adding to his collection, Kanie checks out online shops overseas and specialty stores in Ueno.

8. Genuine illustrations by NAIJEL GRAPH comes complete with the wise words of Yoda.

A room tied together with
subdued tones and textures
such as black and wood. The
couple likes to relax here and
watch T.V. or a movie. The black
leather and green couches are
both by the furniture maker
Karimoku. The cute taxidermy
of a jackalope was ordered from
overseas by his wife's friend.

Yuichiro Ito
Yuko Ito
Suginami, Tokyo

The Ito family lives in a large-scale condo with a verdant courtyard and plenty of common facilities. Their living room, which extends out to their private garden, is furnished with a Hans J. Wegner sofa, Bruno Mathsson chair, and antique Scandinavian cabinet, among others. Seasonal flowers and foliage add color to the impressive collection. As we talk in the garden, their friends, who live diagonally above them, peer out to say hello. Comforting and laidback communal living may be one of the many charms of the Ito residence.

What is the most important theme of your lifestyle?
Play hard and work hard. Work and play are equally important to me.

How do you like to spend your day off?
Traveling with my family. We've traveled to Jamaica, the Bahamas, Morocco, Portugal, Italy, the United States, Phuket, Singapore, Cebu Island; we go on trips overseas at least once a year. We enjoy camping and swimming in the ocean during the spring and summer and skiing in the winter. We go on trips to the *onsen* (hot spring) all year round.

What makes you most glad you decided to purchase your current home?
The fact that we made new friends in the condo. Our condo is a very comfortable place to live because we get to interact with people across many generations in addition to people who are raising kids around the same age as ours or who share similar interests."

What is the most important way to spend your time?
I don't like to waste time. Even when I'm just lounging around, I like to do it with intention.

What is the most cherished item in your home?
The family photos we take at the end of each year.

Do you have a favorite interior design brand or store?
Talo, Rungta, and Ozaki Flower Park.

Which item of clothing do you find most useful when coordinating your everyday style?
I don't know if I find it useful but what's important to me are shoes. No matter what kind of shoes, I always brush them once I wear them. I never wear the same pair of shoes two days in a row.

Which fashion brands do you prefer when creating your own sense of style?
I have no particular preference for brands. I'm the opposite: I always like to follow trends and try out a variety of brands.

What do you hope to purchase next?
A bookshelf by Alvar Aalto, a table for my garden, a rug by Isaac Vasquez, a ski helmet, and a Kawasaki Z1 motorcycle.

How do you hone your sense of style?
Always keep your radars on. Commit to many different things and people. Don't hesitate to invest in things, experience different things, and study them.

The Ito family's garden is like a second living room. Ito likes to sit and read on the Lafuma chair next to his wild, flourishing plants. On top, Ito fixes his custom-made bicycle as his daughter plays.

1. A Baule mask adorns the entrance area along with the protective charm created in Hida-Takayama, Gifu prefecture.
2. The bedo mask by the Nafana tribe was purchased at Rungta in Kyodo. It is Ito's current favorite.
3. Noriyo, Ito's friend and photographer, has been taking the family's portrait every year since the birth of Ito's daughter. These photos mark the passage of time, as shown by the dense trees that used to be small shrubs back when the family first moved into their brand-new home.
4. Stools by Alvar Aalto and Scandinavian stools purchased at the Rose Bowl Flea in California are reserved for guests.

Ito's own chair is by Hans J. Wegner, a birthday present from his wife, Yuko.
5. A bracken basket from Okinawa is placed on top of Sori Yanagi's Butterfly Stool, a piece that was purchased 17 years ago at BEAMS.
6. The Ito family gather around the three-seat sofa by Hans J. Wegner, which is excellent for both lounging and sleeping.
7. The cushions are by Barry McGee. Ilmari Tapiovaara stool and a stool made by the Nupe people complete the corner of the room.

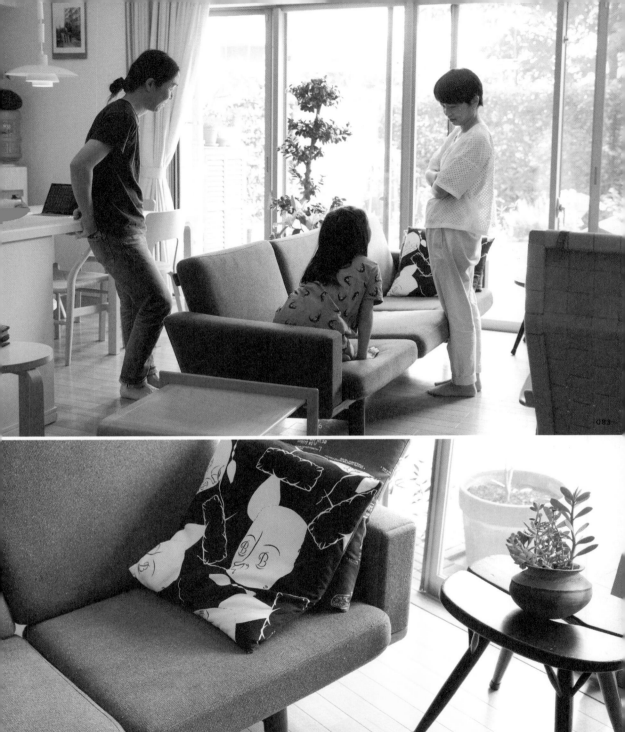

084

⌂ | 👫 | Akishi Sugiura
Abiko, Chiba

A great amount of love went into Sugiura's residence, a serene and traditional Japanese house that he renovated with his friends. "We began by selecting the lumber, then we carved, glazed, and combined them together. To me, creating things is a form of play," Sugiura says joyfully as he gazes at his prized open hearth. As we enter the living room, the fragrance of wood permeates the air, evoking a sense of nostalgia and familiarity. Sugiura lives alongside his *mingei* folkcrafts in a home where every detail has been curated.

What is the most important theme of your lifestyle?
To live somewhere with the right proportion of the countryside. Not too far or close from the urban center.

What is your theme or rule for interior design?
I use various types of wood to create the floor and the pillars. I basically never place anything that does not fit into the atmosphere of the room.

What is your favorite spot in your home and how do you like to spend time there?
The open hearth. The charcoal fire makes the perfect accompaniment to drinking and listening to music. Although I don't have the time to enjoy it too often…

What is the most cherished item in your home?
Nothing in particular, but the head of the family has the responsibility of taking care of the Shinto altar in the home, so I make sure to pray before it every day.

Do you have any collections or things you can't resist buying?
Paper and brushes. I have no idea how many I've purchased. It's hard to tell their quality just by looking at them, so I like to go ahead and buy them.

Do you have a favorite interior design brand or store?
The Matsumoto Mingei Kagu (Matsumoto Folkcraft Furniture). I'm trying to design a custom-made bench right now.

Do you have any advice for people who have trouble keeping a tidy home?
I could use some advice myself. But changing the layout of the room helps me stay motivated.

What kind of fashion style do you like?
I definitely like Fennica's style, which mixes elements regardless of generation or country. The concept of Fennica is "Less global, more local."

What do you hope to purchase next?
I want an oil painting in the room. I like Morikazu Kumagai's work, so I would love a silk screen of his oil painting series.

How do you hone your sense of style?
Try anything and everything that catches your interest.

086

088

3

2

4

1. Energetic killifish swimming inside a large vase welcomed us by the entrance.

2. Handmade folk crafts from different regions of Japan are arranged on a newly installed shelf. The wooden counter beside the kitchen and the Shinto altar have also been made from scratch. "You can arrange wood any way you like, so I can't help but create new things," Sugiura says. Once he starts creating something that interests him, he'll become so absorbed he'll spend the entire weekend or holiday working on it.

3. A relaxing sound echoes through the room every time someone comes and goes through the latticed sliding door. An *inkafu*, a cloth stencil-dyed in the traditional Chinese technique, serves as a sun shade.

4. The high wooden ceiling retains the warm, natural feel of its material. Sugiura chose cedar, Japanese zelkova, and cherry blossom trees for the ceiling panels, walls, and pillars, choosing the material that suits the location best based on the quality of the wood. "What's so interesting about lumber is how the expression of the wood changes depending on its grain or groove," Sugiura says.

090

🏠 | 👥 | Takanori Uchida
Urayasu, Chiba

Uchida has been skiing since he was around two years old, thanks to his parents, who took him along on skiing trips. No doubt his penchant for the outdoors was cultivated as a young boy. Camping, snowboarding, mountain climbing, rafting – many of his hobbies that he picked up as an adult – started from his love of equipment. "I wanted the gear," Uchida says as he surveys the room. The piles of mountain climbing and camping equipment and the storage shed bursting with tents are evidence of his lifelong passion for the outdoors.

What's your hobby?
Skiing, snowboarding, kayaking, camping, mountain climbing, bike riding, tinkering with cars, going to outdoor music festivals.

Do you have any collections or things you can't resist buying?
Outdoor gear at large.

What's your storage rule?
I don't have one. I just store things at random.

What is the most important way to spend your time?
I like to be outside. I want to spend as few days as possible not doing anything.

What is the most important theme of your lifestyle?
Hanging out with friends with similar interests.

What is the most cherished item in your home?
My car and snowboard.

What kind of fashion style do you like?
Half-sleeved shirts and T-shirts for the summer; outerwear and fleeces for outdoor activities during the winter.

Which fashion brands do you prefer when creating your own sense of style?
Mountain Research.

What is your source of information for interior design and fashion?
Go Out, *Begin*, *Brutus*.

What do you hope to purchase next?
A new snowboard.

How do you hone your sense of style?
I think it will come naturally as long as you devote yourself to pursuing what you like.

What's the best thing about working for BEAMS?
Through clothes, my network of people expanded.

What was the most memorable episode you've had at work?
Back when I was working at the stores, I received an order for a wedding. After I took care of it, I received a thank you letter signed personally by the customer.

Caption for page 92:
1. A corner of Uchida's room. Collecting action figures is his hidden hobby. The sale of the action figure of the Iron Giant was delayed multiple times, and he finally purchased it after waiting for two years. Next to it is Iron Man, Gundam, and Andy Warhol.
2. Uchida also loves Snoopy. The Snoopy in the space uniform was a Pocket Doll from 1969.
3. Across from the action figures are an assortment of items indispensable for trekking through the backcountry. "A probe, a beacon, and a shovel are three sacred treasures," Uchida says.

4. A Mammut beacon, essential for climbing snowy mountains.

5. Uchida fell in love with the stylishness of the equipment when he went kayaking with friends. The Feathercraft kayak, ideal for one or two people, was a gift from a friend. He also recently acquired a brand-new inflatable boat. "This one's great for rafting down a rapid stream because it's easy to maneuver."

6. When Uchida goes camping, he likes to leave home by four in the morning and set up camp on site by nine. After that, he spends time eating and drinking; even doing nothing is part of the pleasure. He got hooked on camping when he saw a tent tarp at Asagiri Jam music festival. From there, his passion moved quickly to vintage tents. "The way it feels when you set it up is completely different."

7. & 8. Killifish and lotus flowers just outside the front door.

094

🏠 | 👫 | Maiko Udagawa
Kawasaki, Kanagawa

On weekends, Udagawa and her husband's home becomes a natural gathering spot for friends and family living in the neighborhood. "What's wonderful about living in a one-story flat home is that you get to spending much of the year comfortably," Udagawa muses. A refreshing breeze blows in through the open windows, and mouthwatering aromas of home cooking waft through the sun-filled rooms. It's easy to see why the sunny couple brings people together. Their home teaches us that small happiness that stirs the soul can be found in our everyday life.

Why did you choose to live in this area?
The location is close to the city as well as our respective parents' homes. It's also just five minutes to the river. I like to go running along the riverbank.

What is the theme or rule for your home?
We keep white and brown as our foundational colors and incorporate points of different colors and patterns.

What is the most cherished item in your home?
The welcome board featuring our portrait that an older colleague drew for the occasion of our wedding.

What kind of fashion style do you like?
Basic and simple.

Which fashion brands do you prefer when creating your own sense of style?
BEAMS; Levi's; Yaeca; Engineered Garments; Birkenstock; A.P.C.

What is your source of information for interior design and fashion?
Fashion magazines, blogs, Instagram, Pinterest.

What do you hope to purchase next?
A big house, a big bed, and a big garden.

How do you hone your sense of style?
Absorb many different things, and continue to output as much as you can, too.

How did you begin working for BEAMS?
I've always loved BEAMS BOY, and the store was a place of my dreams.

What's the best thing about working for BEAMS?
You get to meet so many wonderful people who inspire your work.

What was the most memorable episode you've had at work?
When I worked with Chris Gentile, the director of Pilgrim Surf+Supply, his personality and passion inspired so many people to come together and the project was such a success. It reaffirmed the importance of making connections with people and expanding your network.

Plants of various types and sizes line the dining room window. Udagawa purchases cacti, succulents, and air plants wherever she encounters them while out and about on her days off. An enviable display using driftwood and a keen eye for stylish pots.

1. "The breeze flows through the entire house, and it's such a comfortable place to live," Udagawa explains about her home, which is a one-story flat house. Designer clock and memorabilia adorn the small space above the window.
2. On sunny days, Udagawa's pet, a Hermann's tortoise, is allowed to roam free and sunbathe in the yard. He has escaped the yard twice so far, only to be found and brought home by a local elementary school student.
3. Udagawa and her husband both love to surf. Artwork evoking the sea brings visual coherence to the front entrance.

4. A rug purchased in Mexico, the couple's honeymoon destination, welcomes guests at the entrance.
5. A bright bedroom surrounded by windows. The well-loved kilt is by Jessica Ogden, purchased at Fennica.
6. The space is peppered with greens. "Plants are definitely something I'd like to have more of."
7. A treasured welcome board drawn by an older colleague who showed Udagawa the ropes after she joined BEAMS. The portrait is positioned where it can be seen from anywhere inside the room.

100

Takeshi Asami
Tomomi Asami
Suginami, Tokyo

Located on the third floor of the apartment building facing the street, the airy room gets plenty of light thanks to the high ceiling reaching all the way to the loft. The soft green walls were painted by the owner who is also an architect. Inside, Asami shows us each Scandinavian item that surround the room, such as an illustration by the Finnish artist Birger Kaipiainen. "You become interested in something, then you learn about it, and you grow to like it even more." The more you love the things you surround yourself with, the more you enjoy the time you spend with them.

What is the most important theme of your lifestyle?
Keep things that share similar characteristics together (it could be shape, color, country of origin, technique used, or era).

What is the most cherished item in your home?
A mug by Shinman Yamada (I purchased it at BEAMS about ten years ago because I fell in love with the palette and the style.) I drink hot water with this mug every day.

Do you have any collections or things you can't resist buying?
Ceramic ware from the mid-century to today. (Swedish artists Wilhelm Kage and Berndt Friberg; American artist Rose Cabat; Japanese contemporary artists Shinsaku Nakazono, Tsunehisa and Keiko Gunji.) Unique, traditional jewelry by the Zuni people.

Do you have a favorite interior design brand or store?
I like the Finnish company Artek. Everything is simple and relatively light and sturdy. They have many designs with high utility. It's also great that they come in compact sizes with removable and interchangeable parts. It's amazing so many of their designs and shapes have stayed the same for nearly 80 years.

Do you have any advice for people who have trouble keeping a tidy home?
Check in and sort how you feel about the things around you from time to time, and only keep things that you would like to surround yourself with. I think it's best to let go of things that you don't need or that no longer serve a purpose. Every year for my birthday I throw out the same number of things as my age.

What kind of fashion style do you like?
I will always love '70s Saint Laurent and early '80s Vivienne Westwood (Worlds End era).

Which fashion brands do you prefer when creating your own sense of style?
M's Braque, which is also available at BEAMS. I like how there's a sense of humor in their choice of material, detail, and color. It goes so well with vintage clothes too; I purchase a piece or two every year.

Are there any magazines, books, or people that inspire your interior design and fashion?
I always study the interior design of people I admire, not just with magazines but on Facebook and Instagram, as well as old photo books. I follow the U.S.-based Australian artist Ricky Swallow and Takahiro Goko from Swimsuit Department.

What do you hope to purchase next?
Alvar Aalto's vintage cabinet with the L-shaped legs.

How do you hone your sense of style?
Whether it's clothes or interior design, purchase what interests you and search for an ensemble that feels like you. I also think a short cut is to consult people whose style you admire.

1. A decorative dish made in Kitagama, Okinawa; '70s bag by Char from Mexico. Alvar Aalto's coat hanger used as a display hook makes for an innovative idea. "I reference photos of designers' homes often. You can tell a lot about their tastes and they give me a lot of hints." A comfortable room with a medley of vintage items from around the world.
2. The shoe rack in the entrance functions as a space to display illustrations and pottery. A printed sketch by Tomomi's favorite Swedish ceramic artist, Lisa Larson.

3. Takeshi with his favorite ceramics: Lisa Larson's ceramics that they happened upon in Sweden; a finely detailed Berndt Friberg pottery. On the work of the ceramic artist Haruko Kayama: "From the drawing to the coloring, they are more liberated than traditional folkcrafts."
4. Dining table and chair positioned in an airy space. The couple have also purchased plenty of furniture and vintage pieces in Finland, where they traveled to this year.

106

Tomoko Yamaguchi
Meguro, Tokyo

When we entered the white-painted door inside an old apartment building within walking distance from the train station, we discovered an atelier brimming with the smell of paint. Yamaguchi, who lives and paints in this room she rented a few years ago, enjoys a creative life with fellow artists who inspire one another. Art pieces are scattered everywhere inside her home, while plant life, an essential part of her life, serves as a spatial motif. Like she does every other day, she stopped by the local flower shop today to enhance her artistic and relaxed lifestyle all the more.

What is the most important theme of your lifestyle?
To keep my clothes, food, and home in balance. To live in a place where art exists, an environment that invigorates my imagination.

What is your theme or rule for interior design?
I try not to surround myself with only the things I like, so that I don't become "something-esque."

What is the most cherished item in your home?
My artwork.

Do you have any collection or things you can't resist buying?
Confectionery cans. Pins and socks. Monographs of my favorite artists.

Do you have a favorite interior design brand or store?
Watari in Monzen-nakacho. (It's a shop owned by my great mentor.)

Do you have any advice for people who have trouble keeping a tidy home?
I'm not sure what to say since I can't keep things tidy either, but I try to see clutter as a unique character and enjoy it.

What kind of fashion style do you like?
Clothes that reveal the maker's work. A style that tells a story about the wearer.

Which fashion brands do you prefer when creating your own sense of style?
Yaeca, FWK by Engineered Garments, and Susan Cianciolo Studio.

Are there any magazines, books, or people that inspire your interior design and fashion?
Friends (artists and designers) in my orbit give me hints.

How do you hone your sense of style?
It doesn't matter if it's close by or far away—go travel and discover a world you didn't know about.

What is your personal mantra?
Fashion is art for every day. (From the exhibition catalogue of Nakako Hayashi's *You reach out—right now—for something: Questioning the Concept of Fashion.*)

110

1. "I thought it would be great for hanging on a wall or using as a frame," Yamaguchi says of the basket she purchased for around 500 yen. After a lot of thinking, she decided to display shoes inside. Creating storage that you can show off is a trick worth copying.

2. Flowers, which Yamaguchi purchases in flower shops near her home and workplace, add a subtle yet distinctive rhythm to her room. The display on the right exemplifies her taste. "I tried to make it look like an altar," Yamaguchi says with a laugh.

3. Each item in this seemingly miscellaneous room—artwork, strange knick-knacks, and handmade dry flowers—is imbued with Yamaguchi's unique character.

4. There are many items of travel memorabilia, such as a glassware from Finland and a Buddha statue from Thailand. The portrait in the back is Yamaguchi's own artwork. "By painting subjects of various sizes uniformly in a rectangular frame, I tried to delineate the strength of each motif."

111

112

 | Hiroyuki Ota
Suginami, Tokyo

Ota's home feels warm and subtly modern, with textures of bright wood on the floor and walls blending with that of rough concrete. There is nothing to obstruct the flow of space from the front door to the living room, and the uninterrupted view extends out to the garden. From their favorite furniture and plants to wooden DIY furniture, the couple has carefully selected items that speak to who they are. By blending such pieces seamlessly into their life, they have created a truly comfortable home.

What is the most important theme of your lifestyle?
To get plenty of sun.

Why did you choose to live in this area?
It's deep. And it's located close to the city center.

Do you prefer to rent or buy?
I purchased this home. I couldn't find a home that I felt great living in, so I thought, why not create one?

What is your favorite spot in your home and how do you like to spend time there?
Spin round and round in my favorite chair and drink coffee, smoke cigarettes, and read manga.

What is the most cherished item in your home?
Plants (t hey are living things so they are top priority).

Do you have a favorite interior design brand or store?
Moody's in Meguro and Kama-Asa, a Japanese kitchen utensil shop in Kappabashi.

Do you have any advice for people who have trouble keeping a tidy home?
I can't tidy either. I hide my clutter.

What kind of fashion style do you like?
T-shirts and shorts.

Which fashion brands do you prefer when creating your own sense of style?
I don't fall in love with a particular brand. I like all things created with effort.

What is your source of information for interior design and fashion?
I don't really use media as a source of information; I can't feel the writer behind it. Walking around town is most productive and inspiring for me.

What do you hope to purchase next?
I want a cabin inside my home.

How do you hone your sense of style?
Passion! Effort! The desire to make other people happy!

How did you begin working for BEAMS?
I was driven by a singular desire to be popular with women.

What's the best thing about working for BEAMS?
You get to interact with all sorts of people.

"Our priority was to create a refreshing space where we can feel the sunlight and the wind," Ota says. He eschewed curtains so that sunlight can flood the entire room. The tall everfresh tree positioned in the corner imparts a calming mood.

114

1. The plants are all arranged tastefully. The ones hanging from a rail give a sense of depth to the space.

2. "My older colleagues got me into making curry from scratch these days," Yasuda says. Since then, buying spices has become a weekly ritual.

3. The handmade wooden bookshelf was a team effort with his wife, who graduated from art school. The couple is even thoughtful about their selection of tools for their DIY projects, such as the knife manufactured in the U.S.

4. Yasuda purchased the tulip chair by Eero Saarinen when he moved into this home.

5. Kitchenware hangs on the wall. By keeping them neatly arranged, they blend into the space as part of the interior décor.

6. 4Way Canvas by Yard X Sassafras doubles as a make-shift curtain for the bedroom window.

7. A corner dedicated to Mexican goods and accessories, such as tiles and skull figurines. His wife's friend made the wooden stool during their university years.

8. "After tending to it ourselves, we finally managed to get it to this point," Yasuda says of their lawn. Coming up with ideas to arrange plant life in their garden is part of the fun.

6

7

117

8

118

The combination of light wood and gentle gray create an entrance full of warmth. The toned-down colors give coherence to the space while the accessories in the shelf and voluminous plants function as stylish accents.

120

 | | Yosuke Nakazawa
Kokubunji, Tokyo

Have nothing in your house that you do not know to be useful or believe to be beautiful. Those were the words of the father of modern design, William Morris. Even Morris would have felt compelled to heap praises on the Nakazawa residence if he were to visit. Utilitarian objects and interior décors—each deliberately selected without a hint of hesitation—coalesce in this home designed by the architect Makoto Tanijiri, filling it with a perfect sense of balance. The home is a role model for a beautiful and comfortable way of life.

What is your theme or rule for interior design?
My rule is to keep my architectural designs, Scandinavian furniture, and folkcrafts (*mingei*) harmonious so that nothing stands out too much.

What is your favorite spot in your home?
The inner terrace on the second floor.

What is the most cherished item in your home?
The large Japanese antique pot that is also a memento of my grandfather.

Do you have any collections or things you can t resist buying?
Folkcraft dishware and plants.

Do you have a favorite interior design brand or store?
BEAMS, of course.

Do you have any advice for people who have trouble keeping a tidy home?
Instead of trying to hide everything, creatively lay out things you want to show off.

What kind of fashion style do you like?
Classic style for my "on" days. Relaxed style for my "off" days.

Are there any magazines, books, or people that inspire your interior design and fashion?
I read architectural magazines often. I refer to the arrangement of furniture and the plants they use.

What do you hope to purchase next?
A (standing) hammock.

How do you hone your sense of style?
Begin by copying the fashion style of someone you admire or the interior design of a room that inspires you.

What is your personal mantra?
Do what you love and success will follow.

1. The home has all the characteristics of Tanijiri's architecture: a combination of several box-shaped rooms creates the inside of the home. The space is lightly demarcated by the shifting elevations of the floor, a curious layout that offers a different view with every step you take.

2. The second-floor ladder leads to an attic that occupies the entire floor. Nakazawa never designated a particular use for any room at first, but the top floor became a place to keep things that pique his interest, as well as a storage for all his guitars, records, and clothes.

3. The various types of greeneries accent the minimalist room. Though the number of windows is limited, each one, from the skylight to the cutout glass panel in the hallway, has been meticulously designed, ensuring that sunlight streams into the home all year long. A leafy plant thrives at the center of the room.

4. "The only thing I requested was that the home feel free and open. This home was born of an idea to make the inside feel like outside," Nakazawa explains. Since the interior of the home with the exception of the bedrooms is treated as if it were outdoors, he used street lamps to light the hallways. Gardening items naturally blend into the scene as well.

126

🏠 | 👤👤👤 | Masaaki Miyamoto
Setagaya, Tokyo

A retro, wooden house lies at one end of a quiet residential district. When we were ushered inside by Miyamoto, we heard the raucous voices of his roommates. Inside, we saw the floor repaved with plywood, pillars emblazoned with stickers, handmade, one-of-a-kind furniture the roommates made together, and a sundry collection of records. The space, created by freely arranging things with no inhibitions whatsoever, enhances the time spent relaxing with close, like-minded friends.

What is the most important theme of your lifestyle?
To live in a comfortable place that brings many different people together.

What is the theme or rule for your home?
A slightly upscale backstage (LOL).

What is the most cherished item in your home?
The living room table. My roommates and I made it together.

Do you have any collections or things you can't resist buying?
Guitars, effect pedals, skating DVDs, thrift clothes, all sorts of junk.

Which item of clothing do you find most useful when coordinating your everyday style?
Sneakers, of course!

Which fashion brands do you prefer when creating your own sense of style?
Vintage military gear, Vans, Adidas, Hermit.

What is your source of information for interior design and fashion?
All sorts of things, from the magazines sold in convenience stores to photography books and zines. A photo book about Israel is my favorite these days. I also love most books about skateboarding, surfing, and music bands.

How did you begin working for BEAMS?
I was attracted by how the brand handles a breadth of cultures while also bringing out the strength of each to its fullest extent and constantly creating something new.

What's the best thing about working for BEAMS?
I was able to make work into play into a lifestyle.

What was the most memorable episode you've had at work?
Meeting truly cool superiors and bosses.

Miyamoto is largely influenced by street culture, and his room is crowded with things he loves regardless of genre. "Lately I've been into searching for junk at recycle shops. It feels like a treasure hunt."

Film posters and shots of Miyamoto's favorite skaters performing tricks adorn the wall. Weekends are reserved for skateboarding and relaxing with his roommates.

1. A Fender Telecaster, Miyamoto's favorite. Miyamoto is not only a fan of music but also plays in a band. "It's exhilarating to play this guitar at explosive volume."

2. An aquarium found on the street is customized with empty Coke bottles, figurines, and stickers. A fascinating mixture of sensibilities with street influences.

3. "I'm really into cassette tapes right now. I love the retro feel you can never attain from digital music."

4. Respective keys and tools of each resident hangs from hooks on the wall of the shared space.

5. In Miyamoto's hand is a Fender guitar he received from his uncle when he was in grade school. "This is kind of like my root that shaped me and my love of music."

6. Playing video games with friends in the living room is an important moment to chill and relax.

7. The entrance bears the mark of a lively shared home. "I love sharing everything with my roommates. We share not only things but our network of people."

7

132

Stickers add a street vibe to the retro bathroom. Miyamoto and his friends use their hands to refashion their living space to one where everyone can feel at home and enjoy. An attractive lifestyle that values intuition above all.

134

🏢 | 🧍 | Satoshi Nishiwaki
Kawasaki, Kanagawa

Nishiwaki's home showcases his tastes and cultural knowledge, which he honed and cultivated at the countless thrift stores he has been visiting since he was a teenager. There are character goods and toys from overseas, vintage items, golf accessories he refers to for work, and finally a vast number of bandanas that consistently ranks him at the top of the many bandana collectors at BEAMS. Nishiwaki's room perfectly mirrors his personality, a grownup who has retained much of his boyish curiosity and passion. His home has all the creativity and playfulness that characterize a true BEAMS member.

What's your hobby?
Collecting clothes from thrift stores, thrift store hopping.

Do you have any collections or things you can't resist buying?
Bandanas and anything vintage.

What is the most important way to spend your time?
I'm at the turning point of my life, so I try to make sure there isn't anything I don't know about in my fields of interest.

What is the most important theme of your lifestyle?
I like to recreate the feel of the vintage (clothes, accessories, and furniture) shops that have influenced me in my own room. I can live every day surrounded by the things I like.

What is the theme or rule for your home?
I think things you like should always be within view, at least in your own home.

What is your favorite spot in your home and how do you like to spend time there?
I like to sit in a chair and iron my bandanas.

What is the most cherished item in your home?
Bandanas.

Do you have a favorite interior design brand or store?
Talo, Swanky System, Mr. Clean.

What kind of fashion style do you like?
Things that fall somewhere between vintage and regular clothes.

Which fashion brands do you prefer when creating your own sense of style?
Nike, all thrift clothes.

What do you hope to purchase next?
Vintage golf accessories.

How do you hone your sense of style?
You need to hit up a variety of stores, look at all kinds of clothes, and buy them.

What's the best thing about working for BEAMS?
Being able to meet the best talents from each field and work with them.

What was the most memorable episode you've had at work?
I had no interest in golf whatsoever, but by working in BEAMS GOLF I was given the opportunity to produce collaborations with notable brands and present them to customers. I think those items represent what I think BEAMS is all about.

137

"I'm happiest when I'm folding my bandanas," Nishiwaki says. The number of bandanas he owns easily surpasses five hundred. He keeps them beautifully sorted by color and type, from priceless vintage pieces to official sports team bandanas.

1. The countless number of thrift stores Nishiwaki has visited in his life inspire his interior decor. The Stars and Stripes stands in as a curtain. On top of the curtain rail are child size versions of Converse All Stars. He often gives these away to friends.

2. Nishiwaki's bandana collection is sorted inside a cabinet in the center of the room. The collection's sheer volume and immaculate storage system is nothing short of astounding.

3. Vintage banners printed with Peanuts characters.

4. Soft vinyl dolls of Snoopy, purchased at a thrift store,

have gained more character with time. College pennant lunchbox from the '60s.

5. Besides bandanas, Nishiwaki finds L.L. Bean bags irresistible. He has over thirty of them in various sizes, colorways, materials, and eras.

6. Mugs and figurines by Psycho Ceramics. Nishiwaki has been collecting them since he was a teenager.

7. A golf set is a must-have for Nishiwaki, who manages BEAMS GOLF.

8.Nike Golf T-shirts in varied colorways line the closet.

140

🏠 | 👪 | Shoji Kimura
Nagakute, Aichi

"A simple and open space is the theme of my home," says Kimura. With guidance from a designer friend, the exterior, interior, and the furnishing of the home were all based on the ideas of his wife, who used to be Kimura's former co-worker. The plaster wall and the solid wood floor take on a comfortable warmth when the sunshine filters in through the window. The wooden balcony extends out from the living room loft and the first floor, making an ideal space for the family to gather. The expansive view offered by the home makes even the heart feel free.

What is the most important way to spend your time?
Reading books.

How do you alleviate stress?
By reading.

What is the theme or rule for your home?
I try to emulate the qualities of what my friends and older co-workers are doing. I'm still learning.

What is your favorite spot in your home and how do you like to spend time there?
I like to read by the countertop on the first floor. After my family goes to bed, I like to watch movies on the sofa.

What is the most cherished item in your home?
Onta ware pottery and water lily bowl by Koji Sakamoto. An older co-worker introduced me to both items.

Do you have a favorite interior design brand or store?
Favor in Meito district of Nagoya.

Which fashion brands do you prefer when creating your own sense of style?
Scye; Yo's Yo; Sanca; BEAMS.

What is your source of information for interior design and fashion?
Magazines edited by Toru Ukon; styling by Koichiro Yamamoto; blog and articles by Yoshikage Kajiwara; blog and Instagram by Kenjiro Wada, who is my older colleague.

How do you hone your sense of style?
Start by emulating people with a great sense of style. I'm still learning myself.

The scene from midway up the stairs to the second floor. The poster of the Bruce Weber photo exhibit draws the eye. The poster, purchased 18 years ago at the National Portrait Gallery in London, is Kimura's favorite.

143

144

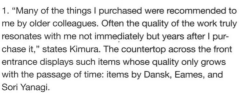

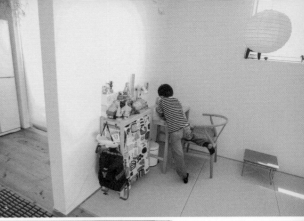

1. "Many of the things I purchased were recommended to me by older colleagues. Often the quality of the work truly resonates with me not immediately but years after I purchase it," states Kimura. The countertop across the front entrance displays such items whose quality only grows with the passage of time: items by Dansk, Eames, and Sori Yanagi.

2. Folkcraft ware that blends into everyday life.

3. Light filters through the small window in the room outfitted with Ryukyu tatami mat. For a limited time, the space doubles as a children's room.

4. Out on the terrace, there is a fir tree that stands slightly taller than Kimura's son. In the winter it functions as a Christmas tree.

5. With a mask by the Dan tribe as the centerpiece, pottery from Shussai, Uezu, and Teruya kiln, as well as ceramics by Lisa Larson are arranged exquisitely atop the large shoe cabinet.

6. An antique basket on top of a rug by the Kuba kingdom, a treasured gift. A sweet air plant sits on a Poul Kjaerholm chair.

7. The lighting in the kitchen is by Poul Henningsen; Onta ware and other pottery are arranged neatly at equal intervals along the plaster wall opening.

A vast bookshelf covers the entire wall. The hallway has enough space for a study and a collection of cacti. Beyond the window is a courtyard where an ash tree and mimosa plant thrive. Plants add a gentle touch of color to the predominantly white canvas of the home.

148

  Takahiko Sato
Shibuya, Tokyo

Walking off the main road in Shibuya, a tall and modern single-family home emerges. The house balances out its rectilinear lines with wood. "I didn't want a home that could not be enjoyed spatially," explains Sato. "I thought this place could be interesting." Inside, a spiral staircase connects the five floors. From the living room with its three wide panels of light-filtering windows to the study on the third-floor mezzanine, the space is structured to enhance the joy of living inside. The many pieces of furniture have each been selected for their time-tested charm. To choose what one enjoys, pass it down, and cherish it—that's a lifestyle to be admired.

What is your theme or rule for interior design?
Along with my photographer wife, I take time carefully selecting items that we find beautiful and we believe will be passed down through the generations.

Do you have any collections or things you can't resist buying?
Autographed books.

Do you have a favorite interior design brand or store?
The last few years, I've become enamored all over again by Memphis, a brand that I encountered back when I was in my teens.

Which fashion brands do you prefer when creating your own sense of style?
I don't have any. But I do like basics that showcase the creator's process.

Are there any magazines, books, or people that inspire your interior design and fashion?
Literature of the past. Art, fashion, interior design, design in general.

What do you hope to purchase next?
Garden, trees, springs, rivers. I'd like to live where man-made things and nature coexist in harmony.

How do you hone your sense of style?
Live the way you like. And commit to what you like.

149

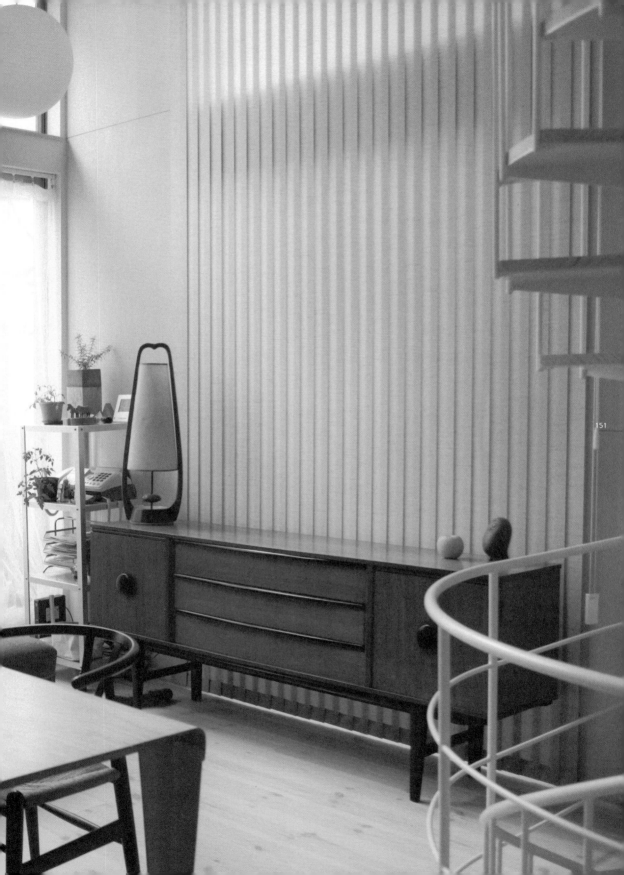

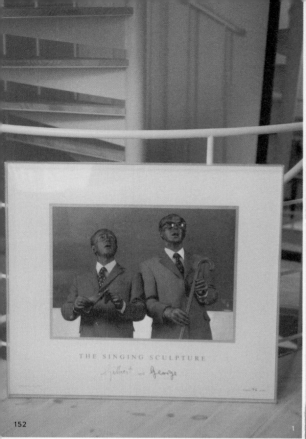

THE SINGING SCULPTURE

1

3

2   4

1. Sato, with a deep knowledge of design and art, owns works by a variety of artists. "This is a piece by the contemporary British artists, Gilbert and George. When I was in my thirties, I used to like artists such as Takashi Murakami whose humorous works have a childishness typical of men."

2. A sense of playfulness can be seen behind the spiral staircase. Flyers for museum exhibits are pinned up with taxidermy magnets as a reminder.

3. Sato keeps his third-floor bedroom simple by having as few things as possible. He explains that, like the living room, the sunlight streaming through the large windows is the highlight of the bedroom. "Large openings to the home provide a way to connect with the outside world, so it's very important to me. I have a small skylight as well, but it's a little too bright and it wakes me up sometimes."

4. Useful and cleverly designed accessories adorn the kitchen. "I'm attracted to items that allow you to see the creator's focus or a new point of view." A beautiful white teapot by Nambu Tekki is a beloved everyday essential.

154

Manabu Kawasaki
Fujisawa, Kanagawa

We hear the sounds of children laughing mingled with buoyant Jamaican music from Kawasaki's living room. While Kawasaki's oldest son toggles between the sofa and the hammock, his twin younger brother runs after Kawasaki's energetic daughter. The wooden deck, extending out from the living room to the open air, makes it feel as if the whole family is camping in the great outdoors. Kawasaki's light-filled home gives each family member space to enjoy each day to its fullest.

What's your hobby?
Music at large (listening, DJing, making speakers). Also cooking, camping, and going to outdoor festivals.

What is the most important theme of your lifestyle?
To always have music and feel its presence in my life.

What is the theme or rule for your home?
Our theme color is green. We don't have any ground rules, but we try to create a refreshing environment.

What is the most cherished item in your home?
Amps and speakers.

Do you have a favorite interior design brand or store?
I don't pay too much attention to brands and just let my intuition guide me. My favorite interior design shops are All Tomorrow's Parties in Sagamihara and Sousuke in Kamakura.

What kind of fashion style do you like?
Simple is best. But these days I mainly wear skateboard or outdoor clothing.

Which item of clothing do you find most useful when coordinating your everyday style?
Mainly caps and other hats.

Which fashion brands do you prefer when creating your own sense of style?
Arc'teryx, all skateboard clothing brands.

How do you hone your sense of style?
Don't be too much of a faddist, cherish your own sense of value, but be aware of other people's eyes on you (LOL).

Caption on page 156:
1. Kawasaki hosts periodic music events with friends. He often listens to techno music in his second-floor room to practice for his DJ gigs. Record player by Technics and mixer by Allen & Heath.
2. Sun Audio amps from the late '70s was a gift from his wife's uncle. The retro chest underneath was made in Denmark in the '60s and purchased at Fusion Interiors in Nakameguro.

3. The star-shaped light was purchased long ago at a lamp store in Kamakura. The lighting in the front entrance and the hallway were all purchased at the same store.

4. The '60s Altec speaker on the right, featured in BEAMS AT HOME 2, was another gift from his wife's uncle. Kawasaki purchased some lumber and made the box himself.

5. & 6. The staircase showcases the sweet artwork by Kawasaki's kids. The second-floor children's rooms are airy and filled with light.

7. The outdoor deck is ideal for BBQs and relaxing on the hammock, as demonstrated on this day by Kawasaki's oldest son.

8. Kawasaki likes to make tacos from scratch with his handmade taco press, pictured here. He cooks what most housewives would prefer not to make, his wife jokes. The kitchen is equipped with a Fostex speaker and NuForce amps so that he can listen to music while cooking. He spent a long time looking for amps that fit into a compact space.

Kawasaki's energetic children are the greatest testament to the comfort of living in this home. Kawasaki and his wife are both from the coastal Shonan area in the southern part of Kanagawa prefecture, so they chose to live nearby in the vicinity of the sea and the mountains. At the back of the kitchen is his wife's beloved Rosiéres gas oven; Kawasaki's speakers hold court in the living room.

158

160

Yuki Sagara
Shinjuku, Tokyo

"Next door is Shinjuku Gyoen National Garden, so it looks like a jungle outside my window. I love the location of my home, which is less than a ten-minute ride from work in my beloved car," explains Sagara, who considers bikes and sweet potato shochu among life's simple pleasures. Although repair work on the exterior of his apartment prevented us from seeing his prized view, Sagara's room, where giant monstera and succulents thrive among furniture made of earthy materials, is an epitome of comfort. A weekend spent here drinking sweet potato shochu—what could be better than that?

What is the most important theme of your lifestyle?
My bike, sake (especially sweet potato shochu), and being surrounded by nature while living in the middle of a city.

What is your theme or rule for interior design?
I rent this apartment so there's a limitation to what I can do in here, but I've installed a wire duct to add extra lighting and improved the atmosphere inside by covering the cheap floor with rugs. I try to collect furniture with good, quality material wherever possible.

What is your favorite spot in your home and how do you like to spend time there?
Reading books or watching a nature documentary while drinking sake on my sofa.

What is the most cherished item in your home?
My plants.

Do you have any advice for people who have trouble keeping a tidy home?
It's your home after all so I think it's fine for it to be a little messy. But I also recommend dividing your storage space so it's easier when you put things back where they belong.

What kind of fashion style do you like?
Something simple and easy to wear that stands the test of time.

Which fashion brands do you prefer when creating your own sense of style?
I don't have a fixed style, but the more I work with a brand the more I grow to love it.

Are there any magazines, books, or people that inspire your interior design and fashion?
Rainer Spehl, a Berlin designer.

What do you hope to purchase next?
If possible, I'd like to get some paint for the walls. Perhaps I'll opt for a removable wallpaper.

How do you hone your sense of style?
Observe people and things with a good sense of style and try to absorb it little by little.

162

1. Sagara has a good supply of dishware in his home. Most of them are Okinawa pottery, which he gradually collected from BEAMS.

2. Sagara likes to spend his days off watching a nature documentary with a shochu in hand. Above the sofa is a world map by The Future Mapping Company. "I put it up with Orskov poster hangers. It's simple yet lightweight."

3. A shelf lined with shochu bottles. "The one I reach for most often is the Rokudaime Yuri from Kagoshima prefecture. It's very fragrant yet goes down easy." A daruma from Zenkoji temple and a plant purchased at Solso Farm keep watch.

4. Sagara made the checkered stools by hand. "Before I started working for BEAMS, I worked as an assistant to a furniture designer in Berlin for about a year. I made these at that time. The fabric was used for slippers but I liked the texture so I decided to reuse them this way."

164

🏠 | 🚻 | Takeshi Shirakawa
Kobe, Hyogo

Hans Wegner Y Chairs, Alvar Aalto stools, benches, and various other chairs are scattered inside Shirakawa's home. "There are only two of us, but we have so many chairs!" remarks his wife, Yuko. The couple loves to entertain guests at home, so they need many chairs. The array of dishware and accessories that have captured Shirakawa's keen curatorial eye also make an appearance when entertaining. Each piece in this home tells a story, and a good time spent gathering with friends adds another story to tell.

What is the most important theme of your lifestyle?
Good food and sake. My wife and I both work, so the time we spend together at home is important.

What is your theme or rule for interior design?
We don't have a particular theme, but we like to make sure that books and bowls are always within reach.

What is the most cherished item in your home?
Works by the artists Koji Toyoda, Keisuke Serizawa, and Shinman Yamada.

Do you have any collections or things you can't resist buying?
Pottery by Shinman Yamada, books, avian figurines.

What is your favorite interior design brand or shops?
Timeless in Nishinomiya and Shukugawa; 6[rock] in Tanba Sasayama; Vivo, Va in Kobe Motomachi.

What kind of fashion style do you like?
In general, I prefer traditional styles. When it comes to accessories and watches, I like quality pieces that get better with age.

Which fashion brands do you prefer when creating your own sense of style?
Orslow.

Are there any magazines, books, or people that inspire your interior design and fashion?
Terry Ellis and Keiko Kitamura from Fennica

What do you hope to purchase next?
A sofa by Børge Mogensen and a hanging scroll by Keisuke Serizawa.

1. Shirakawa's wife, a flower artist working internationally, adds subtle fragrances and accessories to the interior décor. The eclectic pieces are coordinated beautifully and span Japanese and Western tastes.

2. On days off, Shirakawa likes to read with a drink in hand. Books are placed everywhere so that they are always within reach, and his bookshelf is filled with a vast selection ranging from tomes on folk art to beautiful photography.

3. The couple's favorite ceramics representing the various regions of Japan line the cupboard, including those from Kitagama and Shussai Gama kiln, Onta ware, and works by Shinman Yamada. They like to enjoy how dishes change their expression based on the cuisine, enhancing the beauty of each meal.

4. Beloved ceramics by Shinman Yamada are arranged on top of the vintage cabinet made in Denmark. The bowls will adorn the table during new year holidays.

170

🏠 | 👨‍👩‍👧 | Hiroshi Izuhara
Chiharu Izuhara
Hiroshima City, Hiroshima

Izuhara's home is built on a slightly elevated hill surrounded by nature, where the changes of the season can be experienced. Opening the front door, we were immediately greeted by the spacious earthen entryway and the vast, open living room beyond. The interior of the house, with its dominant use of wood, seems to reflect the warm personality of its inhabitants. "I wanted a home where our respective interests can come alive," Izuhara explains. The couple's passion in the outdoors, gardening, biking, and cars can be evidenced everywhere. They are happiest when spending time out on the wooden garden patio.

What is the most important theme of your lifestyle?
A slow life in the countryside.

What is your theme or rule for interior design?
We like to incorporate textures we can enjoy and materials that change with time, such as wood, cloth, and paper.

What is the most cherished item in your home?
The Bruno Mathsson sofa we purchased to commemorate our wedding.

Do you have any collections or things you can't resist buying?
Dishware made of hand-blown glass.

Do you have a favorite interior design brand or store?
1or8, a recycle shop in Hiroshima.

Do you have any advice for people who have trouble keeping a tidy home?
Devote a day to clean one spot in the house entirely.

What kind of fashion style do you like?
I like to ride my bike while wearing a combination of outdoor, surf, and sporty style.

Which fashion brands do you prefer when creating your own sense of style?
Patagonia.

Are there any magazines, books, or people that inspire your interior design and fashion?
We referenced the work of the architect Yoshifumi Nakamura and his book, *Ordinary Houses, Ordinary Cottages*, when we needed inspiration for our home and interior décor.

What do you hope to purchase next?
3171 Bench by Børge Mogensen.

How do you hone your sense of style?
Value what you see with your own eyes, experience and feel in person.

174

1. The living room has no partition whatsoever. The Japanese-style space on the right adds a touch of zen. The rectangular Ryukyu tatami is light and modern instead of overly traditional. The low table along the window is the perfect height for kids to play or write on.
2. A linear and simple exterior. The wooden patio off the large living room window is the couple's favorite spot. A perfect place for a nightcap or shooting the breeze. The planters, tended by Izuhara's wife, are kept in one corner.

3. The sweet blunt-cut bangs on Izuhara's oldest daughter, who is almost a year and a half. Camping and the outdoors have long been a passion of Izuhara and his wife, so they hope to venture together as a family of three this year.
4. A corner for Izuhara's hobbies located right on top of the open ceiling space. Model bikes and cars, as well as architectural books and manga abound. "I like the effort it takes to get here and take what I need," Izuhara explains. It has become his daily habit to sit and read here before going to bed.

178

The BEAMS staff members describe Yasumoto's home as a "Yasumoto folkcraft museum." Even though he was still unpacking from a recent move, the sight of the unbelievable trove of beautiful dishware jumped out at us as soon as we stepped inside. "There's a calming warmth to folkcrafts and pottery," Yasumoto said about his treasures, but he could have also been describing his comfortable home.

What is the most important theme of your lifestyle?
Things from which you can feel the warmth of the hands of their maker.

What is your theme or rule for interior design?
To be without country.

What is your favorite spot in your home and how do you like to spend time there?
The bench by the front entrance. After dinner I like to smoke outside while looking at the killifish, and all the exhaustion from my day blows away.

What is the most cherished item in your home?
My pottery collection, to which I've devoted a lot of time and care.

Do you have any collections or things you can't resist buying?
My wife and I both love bowls so whenever we visit exhibits we can't help but purchase items that we don't have or that are unusual.

Do you have a favorite interior design brand or store?
Nothing in particular, but I like antiques. I like to choose a specific decade, such as the '60s or the '70s, and collect things from in and outside Japan.

Do you have any advice for people who have trouble keeping a tidy home?
When tidying, discard what you don't need. If you are still left with too many things, categorize your room and store things according to each categorical theme.

What kind of fashion style do you like?
American style; things I can wear with ease.

Which fashion brands do you prefer when creating your own sense of style?
In a show of hometown love, Orslow will always be one of my favorite brands.

Are there any magazines, books, or people that inspire your interior design and fashion?
I hardly read any magazines. I look at the photograph of actual participants of the Mingei movement and gather inspirations and ideas from their furniture, way of life, and décor.

How do you hone your sense of style?
Gather clues by looking and touching various things regardless of era or origin.

1. Yasumoto's home overflows with soil, trees, and greenery. An energetic and unique plant hanging from a jute planter hanger.

2. Yasumoto has a vast collection of pottery, though he comments that he never meant to collect so many. This storage space, a converted closet, has an astonishing number of Onta ware and Okinawa pottery slipware.

3. The fragrance of incense and candles that Yasumoto's wife picked out wafts into the entranceway and the rooms, welcoming guests.

4. A plant nestled inside the birdcage by the entrance. The couple's sense of humor can be gleaned in the tiny gorilla figurines decorating the outstretched tendrils.

5. Yasumoto and his wife love old things. Old, cherished items like wooden boxes, baskets, tables, and bottles are utilized in harmony with one another.

184

Kojiro Nagumo
Shibuya, Tokyo

Behind the armchair by Alvar Aalto are wooden trays made by the Ainu people. Made around a hundred years ago, they are carved with a pattern meant to ward off evil. Flower vase also by Aalto. On top of the book, *Katachi, A Picture Book of Traditional Japanese Workmanship*, first published in 1962, is a distinctive white porcelain piece by Taizo Kuroda.

かたち
日本のくらしの形
"KATACHI"

The apartment room of a vintage apartment building built in the Showa era offers a rare, uninterrupted view of Tokyo Tower all the way to Tokyo Skytree, anchored by dense nature beneath. Inside, we found a space of uncommon originality where things that transcend generations and countries— curios and contemporary art, crafts, and design—fuse together. "It's boring to fixate on just one thing. I fixate on not fixating on anything." Nagumo's approach to life is a quintessential philosophy of someone who embodies the essence of a select shop like BEAMS.

What is the most important theme of your lifestyle?
Quality time I spend with my partner, food, conversation, art...

How do you like to spend your day off?
I swim in the morning or go to an antique fair. During the day I relax at a park or go see an exhibit... Then in the early evening I like to go to a bar I know well and start drinking while there's still light outside or invite friends over and enjoy a great meal and sake.

Do you prefer to rent or buy?
Neither. I like to stay free...

What is the most important way to spend your time?
To maintain a balance between the time you think deeply and the time you don't think about anything at all...

What is the theme or rule for your home?
Global, tribal, rustic, antique, vintage, modern, craft, design, art... fusion.

What is your favorite spot in your home and how do you like to spend time there?
That's a secret.

What is the most cherished item in your home?
Instead of a single item, I cherish the composition and harmony of the sum of all parts.

Do you have any collection or things you can't resist buying?
Nothing in particular.

Do you have a favorite interior design brand or store?
BDDW (N.Y.); Galerie Half (L.A.); Antiques Tamiser (Tokyo)

Do you have any advice for people who have trouble keeping a tidy home?
Don't make a mess.

What kind of fashion style do you like?
I don't stick to a particular style.

What is your source of information for interior design and fashion?
The World of Interiors.

How do you hone your sense of style?
To know yourself.

How did you begin working for BEAMS?
It was such a long time ago I've forgotten.

What's the best thing about working for BEAMS?
Perhaps the fact that I'm still working here after thirty years…

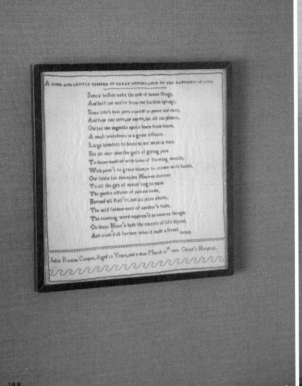

A KIND AND GENTLE TEMPER OF GREAT IMPORTANCE TO THE HAPPINESS OF LIFE.

Since trifles make the sum of human things,
And half our mis'ry from our foibles springs,
Since life's best joys consist in peace and ease,
And few can save, or serve, but all can please,
Oh! let the ungentle spirit learn from hence,
A small unkindness is a great offence.
Large bounties to bestow, we wish in vain,
But all may shun the guilt of giving pain.
To bless mankind with tides of flowing wealth,
With pow'r to grace them, or to crown with health,
Our little lot denies, but Heav'n decrees
To all the gifts of minist'ring to ease.
The gentle offices of patient love,
Beyond all flatt'ry, and all price above,
The mild forbearance of another's fault,
The taunting word suppress'd as soon as thought,
On these Heav'n's bade the sweets of life depend,
And crown'd all fortune when it made a friend.

Julia Rosina Cooper, Aged 12 Years, and a mos March 21st 1840. Christ's Hospital.

1

3

BEN NICHOLSON

THE INSPIRED HOME

MOLLINO POLAROI

2

4

JAPANESE GARDENS

CALDER
ART AND ARTEFACTS
of the Pacific, Africa and the Americas   Steven P
THE JAMES HOOPER COLLECTION

Irving Penn   PASSAGE

ART OF THE ANCESTORS ANTIQUE

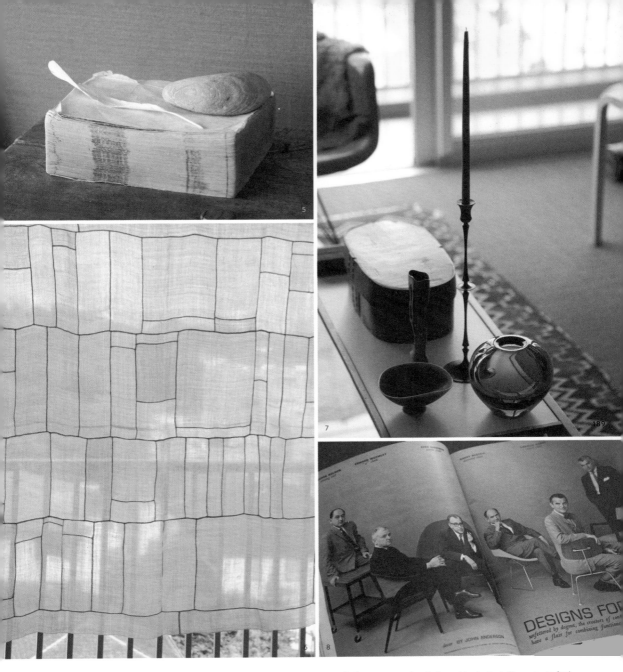

1. The British sampler, featuring virtuous Christian phrases, was made in the 19th century by a thirteen-year-old girl who was practicing embroidery.

2. Arrowheads from the stone age, discovered at an antique market, are arranged like an installation.

3. Peeking behind the Chiavari chair, which set the foundation for Gio Ponti's masterpiece, is a window cut out from a building in India built over a hundred years ago.

4. Nagumo's favorite visual books, a black box from Thailand, and Berndt Friberg pottery are displayed in the corner of the room.

5. A Hawaiian rock and a dictionary from the Edo era with a missing cover are treated as objects that allow you to feel the progress of time. A feather carved from a deer's antler is by the sculptor Masaya Hashimoto.

6. Patchworked fabric known as Pojagi from the Joseon dynasty of Korea. Made of white hemp cloth, it catches the wind when draped by the window, offering a refreshing, cool visual.

7. The Milo Baughman coffee table from the 1950s was purchased twenty years ago. The candlesticks by the American artist Ted Muehling is used on a daily basis. "The gray candles by Creative Candles are the perfect shape for these candlesticks."

8. A *Playboy* magazine from the 1960s featuring a photo of renowned midcentury designers including Charles Eames.

9. A stool hand-carved from a single tree was made by the Bamileke people of Cameroon. "When I found this scaled-out piece six years ago, I was so astonished that I purchased it on impulse." On top of photography books by the legendary American modern photographers Alfred Stieglitz and Walker Evans sits an old photographic slide of an ant and a crocodile paper knife by Svenskt Tenn. In the back is a basket from the Joseon dynasty of Korea.

10. Each piece in the miniature pottery collection by the Swedish potter Sven Wejsfelt is the size of a fingertip.

The glaze on the pieces makes an intricate, beautiful impression.

11. A collection of monographs of artists who have had a profound influence on Nagumo and his worldview: Jean Royère, a decorator representing mid-century French design; Joseph Beuys, a German contemporary artist; Irving Penn, an American photographer.

12. A Buddha statue made entirely of cardboard is the work of the Japanese contemporary artist, Yuji Honbori. When you stand in front in of it the statue appears transparent, showing a ring in its chest.

191

Enshrined next to the sofa is a wooden chest that used to belong to the nomadic people of Northern India. It is covered in llama leather and the white parts are said to be the fur of a snow leopard. On top are silkscreen by the British painter Ben Nicholson, stone sculpture purchased in L.A., and a glass vase by Tapio Wirkkala, among others.

An early 19th-century table used in a farm house in Romania is displayed together with items sourced from around the world, including Africa, Asia, and Scandinavia. The rag or "boro" in Japanese, purchased fifteen years ago, was made from dissembled noragi jackets that were patched together. Some of the quilted pieces are as old as the Edo era.

192

194

The table by Jiro Kimura, made with reclaimed wood, anchors the corner of the room. The photograph of the woman was shot in 19th century China by the British photographer and geographer John Thomson. The lamp is a '50s design by Serge Mouille. Vintage baskets from Rwanda are rare pieces featuring an intricately woven pattern.

196

Tabito Mizuo
Shibuya, Tokyo

Mizuo and his wife requested the concrete walls, bright floor panels, and a large kitchen. The family spends the most time in the roomy and comfortable living room. The painting by the N.Y. artist Kevin Lyons perfectly complements the room. Mizuo purchased it when an exhibit of his work was held at BEAMS T.

198

Mizuno and his wife had plenty of freedom when designing their home, a co-op situated in the heart of Tokyo. From the general layout to the interior details, their home presents an unconventional approach to style and a sense of humor. On this sunny weekend, Mizuo is busy in the kitchen making lunch with his daughter. The conversation between father and daughter escapes into the expansive living room, and beyond it, the terrace opens up to an exhilarating view of the sky and the cityscape below. High above the hustle and bustle, the Mizuo family's life in the city coasts along, unbothered and serene.

What's your hobby?
Playing golf.

Do you have any collections or things you can't resist buying?
Bic lighters and sneakers.

What is the most important theme of your lifestyle?
Comfort.

What is the theme or rule for your home?
A medley.

Do you have a favorite interior design brand or store?
Jasper Morrison.

Which item of clothing do you find most useful when coordinating your everyday style?
Denim.

Which fashion brands do you prefer when creating your own sense of style?
BEAMS (LOL).

What is your source of information for interior design and fashion?
Popeye.

How do you hone your sense of style?
Don't get carried away by what other people are doing.

How did you begin working for BEAMS?
I've always liked BEAMS.

What was the most memorable episode you've had at work?
When Atsuya Furuta, the coach of the Tokyo Yakult Swallows baseball team at the time, hugged me when I worked on the design of their uniforms.

1. Mizuo's home shines with a utilitarian beauty and a sense of humor. The shelving on the wall can double as a bench when guests come over. The Louis Poulsen lamp moves along the railing installed in the ceiling.

2. Photos, artwork, and other records of his daughter's growth can be found throughout the living room.

3. Mizuo is part of the *tokusatsu* or special effects collective at BEAMS. His favorite among the Japanese "superhero team" genre is the Special Investigation Squadron Deka-ranger. His beloved DekaMaster is a side character so its action figure is a rare find.

4. The living room, which boasts an expansive view, has a nook reserved for Mizuo's daughter. She expects to get a room of her own once she enters the upper grade of elementary school.

Mizuo has been collecting Bic lighters ever since an older colleague who worked as a buyer brought him one as a souvenir from overseas. He currently owns about a thousand. The variety of colors and patterns attracted the designer in Mizuo.

Captions for pages 200-201:

5. The big, generous sofa by Eilersen. The colorful, patch-worked cushions were purchased at The Conran Shop and Ikea. Mizuo's daughter likes to practice with the borrowed ukulele.

6. Mizuo has accumulated over 800 CDs of his favorite R&B and black artists since he was a student. The shelf was custom made by a designer to fit his CD cases perfectly.

7. Mizuo's favorite sneaker brand is Vans. The artwork near the front door, like the one in the living room, is by Kevin Lyons.

8. "Will you help me?" "How?" Mizuo's daughter is busy cutting vegetables next to him. Making lunch together is a special bonding time for father and daughter.

204

Kazuhiko Kirita
Mizuki Kirita
Saitama City, Saitama

Kirita's home, located on the upper floor of an apartment building, affords them enough distance from the hustle and bustle of the city. The couple says they've only renovated their home minimally, such as the wallpaper and the floor, but their cozy home shows the character of their peaceful personality. The living room is surrounded with memorabilia while a nice breeze flows through the terrace. And not to be overlooked is Kazuhiko's collection of sweatshirts, which imparts the wisdom that being yourself is the best way to create a comfortable environment.

What is the most important theme of your lifestyle?
To enjoy my clothing, food, and shelter.

What is your theme or rule for interior design?
I prioritize comfort.

What is the most cherished item in your home?
Everything has a meaning so I can't narrow down to just one.

What kind of fashion style do you like?
American casual.

Which item of clothing do you find most useful when coordinating your everyday style?
Work shirts and khaki chino pants.

Which fashion brands do you prefer when creating your own sense of style?
BEAMS, BEAMS PLUS, thrift clothes.

What is your source of information for interior design and fashion?
I get a lot of inspiration from the colleagues working around me.

How do you hone your sense of style?
We all like different things, so I think "what feels like you" is the most important.

How did you begin working for BEAMS?
I was attracted to how the brand, instead of focusing on just the surface of fashion, values the background and the culture behind each item.

What was the most memorable episode you've had at work?
Being a part of the creation of products. It changed my sense of value and how I look at things.

The majority of the accessories in the living room were purchased at BEAMS and in New Mexico. The collection is divided into his and hers. The Eames chair from the '60s was an antique find, used here for working at the computer.

1. 2. 4. Ever since Kirita and his wife moved into their home a year ago, it has seen a steady flow of neighborhood friends and relatives. Their living room has a stylistic coherence, and memorabilia and accessories from the couple's many travels are displayed tastefully. The refrigerator emblazoned with many souvenir magnets.

3. A spacious terrace wraps around the room, with no tall buildings around to obstruct the great view. A perfect place to relax on the weekends.

5. For domestic travels, the couple likes to go to Okinawa. Most of their tableware is Yachimun, a traditional Okinawan pottery.

6. On days off, the husband and wife like to cook together in the kitchen. The dining table in the foreground is by Pacific Furniture Service, the chairs by Emeco.

7. The antique standing light is Kirita's favorite. Its time-weathered character matches the mood of the room, which is best described as a mix of the modern and the foreign.

8. A corner of the sunny living room. The sofa was purchased at Pacific Furniture Service. The table is an antique piece from the '60s by the storied American furniture maker, Lane. On the left, everyday accessories are kept on the built-in work desk.

210

🏢 | 🚻 | Toshihiro Yasutake
Eriko Yasutake
Shinjuku, Tokyo

Yasutake's newly renovated apartment home stands in a section of the Kagurazaka neighborhood, known for side streets and alleys lined with elegant shops tethered to the past. Yasutake and his wife reconstructed the heavily partitioned layout of the home, opting instead for an unobstructed space with exposed concrete, tied together with black, steel furniture. The garden in the back stretches as freely as the interior of the home. The dedicated corner for trinkets purchased on international business trips marks the busy lifestyle of the husband and wife who both work in fashion.

Do you have any collections or things you can't resist buying?
Pitchers and vases, objects that can be easily used to decorate the room. Recently, I'm into metal accessories and items with simple and economical designs.

What's your storage rule?
Use conveniently sized storage boxes that you don't mind showing off instead of large storage furniture.

What is the theme or rule for your home?
When we renovated our home, we took out the partitions to make it a continuous, expansive space. To match this space, we only place furniture with delicate forms or those that we can move around by ourselves. Also, we don't use furniture that stands higher than our line of sight. Hanging items from the ceiling is also a good way to accent the space.

What is the most cherished item in your home?
Poul Kjaerholm PK-22 armchair; it's a 60th anniversary edition. My wife and I had been looking for a PK-22 for a long time when we learned that they were releasing a 60th anniversary model with gray nubuck leather. We decided to purchase it instantly.

Do you have a favorite interior design brand or store?
Graphio/büro-stil, Granpie, Eguchi Yohinten

Why did you choose to live in this area?
This area is interesting because you see a mix of historical and new concept stores. Being in the heart of the city also means it doesn't take long to go anywhere.

What kind of fashion style do you like?
A style that reflects the current era somewhat. Also, a style that is a little dapper.

What is your source of information for interior design and fashion?
Dealer's Choice.

How do you hone your sense of style?
Listen to what the professionals in various genres have to say and process those ideas into a form that satisfies you. Then, try them on yourself.

How did you begin working for BEAMS?
I love being steeped in the world of fashion that I had dreamed about when I was young.

What was the most memorable episode you've had at work?
I used *BEAMS AT HOME* when I proposed to my wife.

The space on the other side of the sliding door is a study. The space is just small and cozy enough to invite focus. The centerpiece of the living room is the 60th anniversary edition of POUL KJAERHOLM PK 22, beloved for its design and the texture of nuback leather. The T.V. wires are covered with mechanical-looking pipes.

213

214

1

3

4

2

5

1. An old sign from an East German eyeglass factory decorates the hallway to the living room. Purchased at General View.

2. The sturdy black door by the front entrance opens to the spacious living room with a view of the verdant garden. The garden is sheltered from outside view, so there is no need for curtains or blinds.

3. Displayed on the floor is a poster by the photographer Jiro Konami, one of Yasutake's favorites.

4. Light floods the room from the open window facing the garden.

5. The walk-in closet was specially designed to accommodate the couple's large volume of clothes. The closet connects to both the bedroom and the front entrance, allowing for ease of movement during busy mornings.

6. The entire wall separating the bedroom and the hallway functions as a storage space for shoes.

7. Antique dart board, a clock, and a steel fan, which was purchased for its unique, industrial features.

8. The bedroom, accessible from the living room via a rotating door, features sisal floors, which gives the room a relaxed vibe. Magazines and books and ceramic wares by Adam Silverman decorate the area around the window.

7

215

8

216

The large, rectangular tiles of the softly illuminated bathroom leave a lasting impression. The showerhead is by the German brand Grohe, the enamel bathtub was also ordered from the German brand Kaldewei. The natural stones used on the floors emphasize the hotel-like luxury.

218

🏠 | 👫 | Akira Sugano
Kobe, Hyogo

Escaping the hustle and bustle of Sannomiya, the family moved to a more ideal environment for children. When choosing a place to live, Kanno wanted to live close to the sea, taking advantage of the landscape of Kobe. It has been a year and a half since he and his family moved here. The array of vintage, natural, and well-loved items makes the comfortable home feel as if they've lived there for far longer. By learning to be calm and quiet in a place full of trees and nature, the family has learned that human beings are also part of nature.

What is the most important theme of your lifestyle?
To be close to the sea, to live where you can see the sea.

What is your theme or rule for interior design?
A living space where trees and greenery take center stage.

What is the most cherished item in your home?
Vintage textiles.

Do you have any collections or things you can't resist buying?
Indigo-dyed textiles and army gear.

Do you have a favorite interior design brand or store?
Like Like in Kobe; 102 in Kobe

Do you have any advice for people who have trouble keeping a tidy home?
Line up the things you like.

Which fashion brands do you prefer when creating your own sense of style?
Orslow. It's not a brand, but I like thrift clothes.

Are there any magazines, books, or people that inspire your interior design and fashion?
Brutus magazine. I get hints and ideas on fashion from people I see out on the town and in stores.

How do you hone your sense of style?
Start out by copying things that you like.

What is your personal mantra?
Don't place limits on yourself. Challenge yourself no matter how old you are.

221

224

🏢 | 🚻 | Yui Koyano
Setagaya, Tokyo

To make whatever they can on their own. Koyano's home, whose style has always been driven by this straightforward philosophy, is tied together by DIY furniture and populated with timber waiting for its turn to be used and random fragments of material leftover from past projects. There is a joy in creating one's own unique space little by little, just as there is joy in gazing at a thriving plant or sharing a delicious meal. Koyano's home is a testament to how life's simple everyday pleasures are enough to make one's heart skip a beat.

What is the most important theme of your lifestyle?
A life surrounded by plants and delicious food.

How do you like to spend your day off?
Prepare and eat a well-balanced breakfast.

What is the theme or rule for your home?
Our theme is "West Coast" but we deviate slightly from it. We try to create what we can on our own.

What's the next theme you hope to have in your home?
A simple, minimalist home.

Do you have any collections or things you can't resist buying?
Air plants, succulents, big trees.

Do you have a favorite interior design brand or store?
Rungta in Kyodo.

Do you have any advice for people who have trouble keeping a tidy home?
Periodically invite guests over to your home.

Which fashion brands do you prefer when creating your own sense of style?
BEAMS.

What is your source of information for interior design and fashion?
Books and magazines about Hawaii.

How do you hone your sense of style?
I'd love to ask people this question too, but for me, it's to "visit, observe, listen, and touch."

How did you begin working for BEAMS?
I've always admired BEAMS staff, products, and the company itself.

What's the best thing about working for BEAMS?
I have gotten to know colleagues who always encourage and support me.

What was the most memorable episode you've had at work?
One time I assisted a female customer who was blind.

Before she left the store, she took my hands in hers and said, "thank you." I was so happy a customer took my hands like that; I still remember it clearly.

Captions for pages 228:
1. A plethora of plants sits by the large window, which fills the entire living room with light. An older colleague at BEAMS taught Koyano about Rungta, a furniture store in Kyodo, and it has since become her favorite as well.
2. For lunch, Koyano's husband cooked his trademark pasta dish: Bolognese seasoned with salt and prepared without tomatoes. The couple likes to use seasonal ingredients so that they can enjoy the four seasons together through their meals.

Koyano's husband prepares lunch. "We both love cooking and drinking sake, so we invite friends over periodically," Koyano says. A happy home is one where a delicious meal is always on offer. Sharing a drink after dinner is something the couple also looks forward to every night.

227

228

The apartment feels expansive thanks to the seamless structure that connects the living and dining rooms and the kitchen. The high ceiling upstairs was also a big factor when the couple decided to rent this duplex apartment. The upstairs rooms are used as a bedroom and a closet.

230

🏠 | 👩‍👧‍👨 | Takahiro Nakai
Niiza, Saitama

In Nakai's home, the things he enjoys most and wants to use for a long time are kept in a simple and humble fashion. Sunshine streaming in through the double-height ceiling emphasizes the brand-new ivory interior of the home even more. "I hope the times we spend here will leave their mark on the home," Nakai says. Even the wear and tear that will naturally occur with the progress of time are something to look forward to when considered as records of his daughter's growth and the family's shared history.

What's your hobby?
Traveling or visiting museums with my wife.

Do you have any collections or things you can't resist buying?
Ever since we built this home my wife and I became hooked on collecting chairs.

What is the most important theme of your lifestyle?
Communication as a family. My favorite feature of this home is its structure, because no matter where you talk from, your voice will reach someone.

What is the theme or rule for your home?
To keep the number of things you own under control.

Do you have a favorite interior design brand or store?
I don't have a particular store, but when we were building this home I went to Osaka from Tokyo a number of times just to visit Truck Furniture.

What kind of fashion style do you like?
I like authentic items, but right now it's all about rough and casual style that allows me to move.

Which fashion brands do you prefer when creating your own sense of style?
I like Scye and Haversack; I'm attracted by clothes that are authentic yet contemporary.

What is your source of information for interior design and fashion?
Popeye, *Begin*, and *Houyhnhnm*; and surprisingly, I learn a lot by listening to the radio.

How do you hone your sense of style?
I think you need to spend some time shifting your focus outside of clothes.

What's the best thing about working for BEAMS?
At work and in my personal life, I get to interact with various places, things, and people.

What was the most memorable episode you've had at work?
I have so many memories, but what comes immediately to mind is the press preview event we hosted overseas. Experts from various departments came together to create the world of BEAMS, and the look of anticipation on our customers' faces as they entered the store left an enduring impression on me.

233

Nakai's wife majored in architecture and always wanted to design her own home. The couple constructed the double-height ceiling and large windows so that they would not have to depend on artificial lighting during the day. The bedroom was also designed carefully in the image of a foreign hotel room; the bedroom window is positioned so that the starry sky is all they see when they look up at night.

2

1. The mezzanine, which overlooks the dining room, is Nakai's work space. The lack of walls, which allows him to see his wife and daughter downstairs, is a design feature that reflects his wish to prioritize family communication above all. When his daughter becomes older, he plans to turn this into her study nook for doing homework. Alvar Aalto chairs by Artek. The light filtering through the window brings comfort and warmth to the space.

2. Simple yet curated furniture adorns the room. Since Nakai and his wife are both from the Kansai region of Japan, they purchased the custom-made table and sofa from Osaka's Truck Furniture. The living room was specially designed to accommodate the size of the sofa.

3. A gallery-like corner on the second-floor. The picture by Kurry called No Border, purchased at Noiseking, was selected as a message for his daughter in the future.

4. Vintage chairs by Ilmari Tapiovaara. "These chairs are meaningful to me because it was the first time I purchased chairs as a pair, since I knew I was about to start a family. I'm thinking about adding one more when my daughter gets bigger."

5. Homemade meals prepared by Nakai's wife look as decadent as they taste.

6. The bathroom is a model of meticulous consideration. After much debate, the tiles were carefully selected for their width and texture.

A simple kitchen coordinated in white. On the shelf are unassuming yet beautiful tableware purchased at Fennica: Onta ware, Ittala, and Marimekko. The set of white enamel baking dishes from Noda Horo is treasured for their versatility—they can be directly heated over open fire or used as storage containers.

238

 | | Mika Maruyama
Suginami, Tokyo

A solitary house stands in a corner of a residential district located off a main street. A pleasing staircase made of natural wood leads to the living and dining room filled with Maruyama's favorite plants and *mingei* folkcrafts, as well as designer chairs that her husband likes to collect as a hobby. The couple's pet dog and star of the home, Mumu, welcomes us in. The close-knit family of three (two humans, one dog) cohabits this tranquil space, where midcentury and Japanese modern mix together to create its own unique uniformity.

What is the most important theme of your lifestyle?
I was born in Sendai and grew up in Tokyo, so Kichijoji is an ideal town for me: it's got the right amount of urban and country atmosphere. The Inokashira Onshi Park nearby allows me to stay close to nature, which I love.

What is your theme or rule for interior design?
My home is mostly filled with my husband's collections. The house rule is to avoid cluttering the living room as much as possible. I like flowers and plants so arranging and displaying them is part of my hobby.

What is your favorite spot in your home and how do you like to spend time there?
I'm always comforted by the view of the ceiling as seen from the sofa in the living room. I love gardening in my little garden and I look forward to seeing different flowers bloom every season.

Do you have a favorite interior design brand or store?
I highly recommend Fennica. I also like Tumikusa, Rozan, El Sur, and Hana101.

What kind of fashion style do you like?
I love following trends in general, so I'm always aware of what's in. But I don't like wearing the same brand head to toe, so I enjoy coming up with original ways to style my clothes every day. I also love pearls, so I think I always have them on. My name, Mika, contains the Japanese kanji character that symbolizes "pearl" so I feel calmer when I have pearls on. But I just wear whatever suits my mood that day!

Which fashion brands do you prefer when creating your own sense of style?
BEAMS BOY, Sacai, Chanel, Hermès, pearls, vintage clothes, denim. BEAMS is indispensable for my lifestyle and fashion.

Do you have any magazines, books, or people that inspire your interior design and fashion style?
Audrey Hepburn and Coco Chanel are my idols for life.

How do you hone your sense of style?
You have to know yourself. Put out as many antennae as possible and absorb a lot of information. You can't win against people who take the time to go to different places and see new things. Studying is important. I'm always invigorated by conversations with my friends; they are my source of learning.

What is your personal mantra?
Empathy.

240

1. Greenery is placed tastefully around the home. A reflection of Maruyama's love of gardening, the abundant plant life found in the kitchen or the side of the staircase creates a comforting atmosphere.

2. The interior of Maruyama's home, which was custom-designed by an architect, is built entirely of Japanese red pine. The home is so clean and well cared for that it's hard to believe it is twelve years old. Adjacent to the living room is a Japanese-style room with no partition, a perfect space for relaxing.

3. A veritable museum of renowned design chairs, which Maruyama's husband collects as a hobby. Pictured here is a chair designed by Norman Cherner, one of the representative designers of American midcentury designs. It has been three years since Mumu joined their family and since then the living room has been turned into his playground. Harry Bertoia chair, a rare masterpiece, is the family's favorite.

4. The corner of the Japanese-style room dedicated to Mumu's toys. Mumu likes to play indoors as well as at the Inokashira Onshi Park nearby.

241

242

 Yosuke Sekine
Shinagawa, Tokyo

The home is neither European nor American, masculine nor feminine. "I wanted my daughters to feel relaxed, so instead of creating it from a grownup standpoint, I wanted the room to feel more neutral," explains Sekine. The oak floors finished with natural oil and the antique and vintage furniture, lighting, and accessories are all materials that will change with the ebbs and flows of time. As parents, Sekine and his wife value a life in which they can enjoy the passage of time as their two daughters grow up.

What is the most important theme of your lifestyle?
I'm always conscious of how my family can live comfortably. I only add a small bit of my own interests and tastes within that framework.

What is the most important way to spend your time?
Being with my family.

What is the theme or rule for your home?
I don't have any assertions or rules. I purposefully refrain from having one. I like to go with how I feel at the time instead of limiting myself to any format. I like things that get better with age, so I have many antique or vintage pieces.

What is the most cherished item in your home?
If I were to pick something I would choose memorabilia from our time together as a family or gifts from my children (you can always buy material things, after all).

Do you have any collection or things you can't resist buying?
Things related to Kurt Cobain.

Do you have a favorite interior design brand or store?
Interior design stores along Meguro-Dori Street and Seasaw in Mishuku.

What kind of fashion style do you like?
I like things that age well, things with character and texture. My style runs the gamut, from high fashion to thrift clothes.

What is your source of information for interior design and fashion?
General View, an online select shop.

How did you begin working for BEAMS?
For me, BEAMS was the coolest. I was lucky to have been accepted.

What was the most memorable episode you've had at work?
There are so many, but I always think it's amazing that I get to work with James Iha (the former member of The Smashing Pumpkins) through my association with the brand Vaporize.

True to the family's wish to cherish their meal times, the Sekine family decided to incorporate a dining space inside the kitchen while they were renovating their home. The kitchen, made to function like a cafeteria, stands distinct from the living room. The new kitchen helps the family use their time more efficiently and conversations flow naturally as they gather around the table.

With white as the foundational color, each detail in the kitchen has been carefully selected by the couple. The stainless-steel gas oven by the French brand Rosières boasts a simple, efficient design, and its glass top cover is a marvel of utilitarian beauty. The oven was a gift from his wife's friend.

245

1. Sekine has been collecting photos of Kurt Cobain published by the company rockarchive.com ever since BEAMS began handling them. Now that he has a family, he displays the photos in a small gallery-like corner on the second-floor landing (P. 244).

2. Thanks to the natural materials used for the floor, the children are free to stretch out. The floor uses natural oak finished with a natural veneer by the German company Osmo.

3. Sekine's younger daughter loves the character Shizuka from the Japanese manga series Doraemon.

4. The children's room has a girlish feel. The Lego Cinderella castle undergoes a constant scrap-and-build process in which Sekine's older daughter builds and his youngest destroys.

5. The black photo frames give family portraits visual coherence, blending them seamlessly into the room.

6. The bookshelf was custom made when the room was being renovated.

7. Most of the furniture is vintage. The living room maintains a balance so that it never feels too grownup or childish; the priority is for everyone in the family to feel comfortable.

248

🏠 | 🚹🚺 | Takeshi Imamura
Yokohama, Kanagawa

Imamura's home is built on top of a hill overlooking Yoko-hama, a city of hills. Both the exterior and interior of the home comprise a sophisticated fusion of Japanese and modern styles, and the window offers a commanding, expansive view. At the entrance of the spiral staircase in the center of the home hangs a handwoven textile, the "fabric of life," made in the Kuba kingdom of Central Africa. The textile and the Japanese mise-en-scène, such as lattice de-tails, convey a mysterious sense of harmony. Imamura can usually be found relaxing on the Mexican rug spread out in the Japanese-style room on the second floor. The taste of shochu, accompanied by his wife's cooking, is exceptional.

What is your theme or rule for interior design?
Instead of worrying about the bigger picture, I just collect what I like one item at a time.

What is the most cherished item in your home?
The sofa.

Do you have any collections or things you can't resist buying?
Bandanas and socks.

Do you have a favorite interior design brand or store?
Hike, Pacific Furniture Service, Talo.

Do you have any advice for people who have trouble keeping a tidy home?
Divide the storage you want to show and storage you want to hide and use both of them wisely.

What kind of fashion style do you like?
Basics deconstructed in my own way.

Which fashion brands do you prefer when creating your own sense of style?
M's Braque; MP di Massimo Piombo; Class.

Are there any magazines, books, or people that inspire your interior design and fashion?
Citizens of the 20th Century by August Sander; *Cheap Chic.*

What do you hope to purchase next?
A chair.

How do you hone your sense of style?
Interact with films, books, and music that stir your imagination.

What is your personal mantra?
Value your intuition.

1. In the corner of the living room is a shelf by Ou Ba-holyodhin, which is also available at BEAMS. The shelf, composed of stackable parts in reverse C shapes, can be arranged and combined in different ways. Imamura keeps his beloved Western books here. The sofa, glimpsed here, was made in Denmark in the '70s, and Imamura fell in love with it at first sight when he found it in Hike in Nakameguro. Pillow covers by the renowned Finnish textile designer Johanna Gullichsen were purchased at Fennica. The covers are also used as a tablecloth on the dining room table.

2. The exterior of Imamura's house weaves a stunning contrast of black and white stucco. A hint of playfulness can be gleaned in the red mailbox standing in the midst of greenery.
3. A framed poster of the 1972 black-and-white silent film *Metropolis* adorns the top of the shelf.
4. The dining room is a favorite gathering spot for the couple. Imamura's wife loves the Western iron kettle, painted bright red.

254

Kensuke Ido
Adachi, Tokyo

"Nothing beats this view," muses Ido as he shows us into his spacious room. The wind sweeps in through the large windows, opening up to a vast view of both the Arakawa and the Sumida rivers. After brewing some coffee, we sit around the balcony. For Ido, sipping coffee while taking in the view and listening to the laughter of his two rambunctious sons is a treat. Even in the middle of the city, here it is possible for the family to spread out amid nature. We can think of no greater happiness than a home that allows you to feel as if time slows down just for you.

What is the most important theme of your lifestyle?
To live in an environment close to nature.

What is the most important way to spend your time?
To spend time with my kids. They grow up quickly, so the time is now.

What is the theme or rule for your home?
I want my home to have a DIY feel. I'm thinking about actually building more walls or shelves by myself, though right now I'm still just thinking about it. I like spaces that feel comfortable. More plants the better, too.

What is your favorite spot in your home and how do you like to spend time there?
My balcony. In the morning I like to drink coffee there. At night I drink sake. I always invite friends over, set up a table and chair, and talk with them on the balcony.

What is the most cherished item in your home?
A table by Pacific Furniture Service. I make sure to wax it from time to time. Also, my Yamaha acoustic guitar. I inherited it from a high school friend.

Do you have any collection or things you can't resist buying?
Thrifted gray sweatshirts and denim. I'm not partial to any era or brand, but I buy them if I find them in sizes and silhouettes that are hard to find these days, or if the material or the damage appeals to me.

What kind of fashion style do you like?
I like easy- to-wear styles and thrift clothes. But I don't wear thrift clothes from head to toe; I often mix and match them with sophisticated items.

Which item of clothing do you find most useful when coordinating your everyday style?
Converse. They go with any style. Even with the same design you can coordinate them in a variety of ways depending on the material or color.

What is your source of information for interior design and fashion?
I read a majority of the men's fashion publications. Online I look at things like *eyescream.jp* or *Houyhnhnm*. I check most things due to the nature of my work. For interior design, I refer to the homes of my friends or colleagues. When it comes to fashion, it's important that I can wear them without trying too hard, but my greatest inspiration is the BEAMS buyers.

What's the best thing about working for BEAMS?
I have older and younger colleagues and those in my age group who all inspire one another. It's just so much fun, both as work and play. I consider it a great blessing in my life.

The scenic balcony proves to be a great spot to raise plants as well as turtles. Ido's younger son is in charge of watering the plants every day.

The large hammock by Hammock2000 is perfect for their spacious living room. The idea of installing the hammock was inspired by Ido and his wife, who love the outdoors. They are looking forward to camping as a family soon.

258

1. The shelf in the living room is reserved for sentimental items as well as products Ido has worked on. The retro vacuum tube radio was a gift from his parents. Built in the Showa era and manufactured in Japan by Tokyo Denki Sangyo, it is still in working order and has a unique sound full of character. On the upper left is a pair of GM engineer boots by Shantii, Jun Murakami's brand.

2. The Pentax film camera and projector work as interior décor that enhance the mood of the room. The camera, which Ido's wife used in the past, will be dusted off and deployed the next time the family goes camping.

3. The pair of American-made Vans was a celebration gift from Suguru Kumasaka, the owner of the select shop Fridge in Setagaya, on the occasion of the birth of Ido's firstborn son.

4. The living room, and in particular the Unico sofa, is a gathering spot for the family. Ido carefully handles the acoustic guitar, a precious inheritance from his friend.

260

Kyoko Sakaguchi
Setagaya, Tokyo

It takes us only a minute to walk from the train station to Sakaguchi's designer apartment. When we ring the intercom, her friendly dog Stella is the first to welcome us. Inside, light and wind filter through the huge window that stretches all the way up to the ceiling. Green plants grace the dining room, where Sakaguchi and her husband eat every day around their favorite table. Sakaguchi's compact apartment brims with countless precious things, such as a iron kettle inherited from her grandmother, an artwork created by her sculptor uncle, and a dresser that she has been using ever since she was a little girl. Sakaguchi's life is one filled with the love of her family.

What is the theme or rule for your home?
To have a large amount of greenery. My interior décor is still a work in progress, but when I purchase an item I make sure that it's something I can use for a long time and enjoy seeing it change throughout the years.

Do you have any collections or things you can't resist buying?
Glassware. Right now, my favorite pieces are the glass and pitcher that I purchased at Tumikusa in Kichijoji. I also use the Peter Ivy glasses often.

Do you have a favorite interior design brand or store?
D&Department. I bought a bookshelf there.

What kind of fashion style do you like?
My basic style is simple. Once I figure out what I like or looks good on me, I like to express that through my clothes.

Which item of clothing do you find most useful when coordinating your everyday style?
Pearl earrings and jeans. My favorite pair is from A.P.C. I'm breaking them in carefully.

What is your source of information for interior design and fashion?
I like the blog written by the illustrator Garance Doré. The grownup French taste is lovely. I also like the Man Repeller because it's unique and interesting.

What do you hope to purchase next?
A house and a car. Ever since a friend told me I'd look good in a Nissan Rasheen, I've been curious.

How do you hone your sense of style?
Experience. You also need to make mistakes repeatedly.

What's the best thing about working for BEAMS?
Getting to meet people who truly love fashion. It made me realize how that passion can become a driving force for your work.

What was the most memorable episode you've had at work?
The opening of each of our overseas branches that I've been involved in. A huge amount of staff both in and outside the company contribute to the opening, which only heightens our happiness on the day of the launch. It's also a moment when I realize how many people support me in what I do.

The Sakaguchi family—two humans and one dog—live alongside furniture that they know they will cherish for a long time. They also love spending time outside on the wooden deck during warmer seasons. Sakaguchi's husband is in charge of brewing coffee. Today, he makes a delicious cup with beans from Blue Bottle Coffee.

264

3

BISLEY

2   4

1. A collection of memories arranged on the shelf by the front door. A branch, found while walking around during a trip to Aomori prefecture, is placed inside an Onta ware flower vase. Stella's baby teeth are kept in a small bowl, a souvenir from Ishikawa prefecture.
2. Sakaguchi's favorite shoes, including pairs from Christian Louboutin and J.M. Weston, are stored in shoe boxes. Polaroid snapshots help you see what's inside at a glance.
3. A fish mobile sways in the bedroom. The dresser, which Sakaguchi has been using since she was a child, changes and deepens its character with each passing year.

4. A bear figurine and snow globes purchased on business trips line the top of the Bisley file cabinet.
5. The entrance to the bathroom area as seen from the kitchen. Accessibility is part of the charm of the apartment's layout. The iron kettle in the kitchen is a gift from her beloved grandmother.
6. The comfy sofa is by Tendo Mokko, a low table by Kartell, and a rug by the Finnish brand Johanna Gullichsen.
7. Even shoes and tableware can be stored together as long as everything is painstakingly cleaned and cared for.

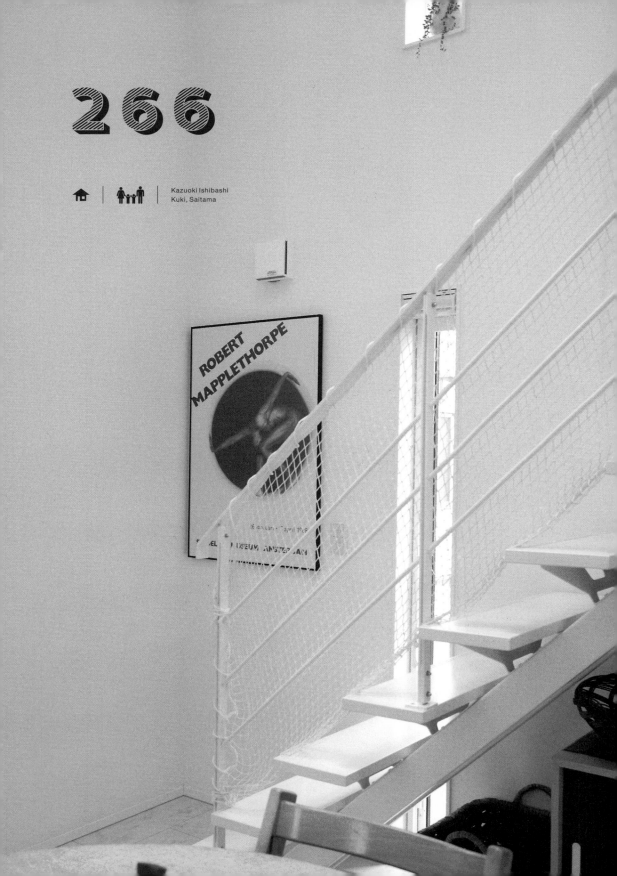

266

🏠 | 👪 | Kazuoki Ishibashi
Kuki, Saitama

The Ishibashi family lives in an idyllic landscape dotted by farmland. Ishibashi and his wife, together with their two children, live in a modern, single-family home. A playful array of designer furniture and Okinawan folk crafts pop in their monochrome living room, compete with few accent colors and a high, open ceiling. Mingling with the joyous cries of Ishibashi's children, the comfortable atmosphere brings his family together each day.

What is your theme or rule for interior design?
Nothing in particular. If I were to list one thing it's to keep my room from getting too cluttered.

What is the most cherished item in your home?
Alvar Aalto cabinet designed exclusively for Fennica.

Do you have any collections or things you can't resist buying?
Salt glaze pottery bowls by Tomoo Hamada.

Do you have a favorite interior design brand or store?
Fennica. We buy the majority of our furniture there.

Do you have any advice for people who have trouble keeping a tidy home?
Declutter.

What kind of fashion style do you like?
I like most of American casual style.

Which fashion brands do you prefer when creating your own sense of style?
Sanca. Battenwear, known for their basic and sporty style, is also one of my favorite brands these days.

What do you hope to purchase next?
Valve Lamp from Gino Sarfatti.

What is your personal mantra?
Go for broke.

267

1

3 271

2 4

1. Cabinet designed by Alvar Aalto, Ishibashi's favorite. With multicolored doors, the cabinet was made to order for Fennica, where he purchased it a few years ago. Displayed on top of the cabinet are many folkcrafts, including pottery from Yomitan, Okinawa.

2. A handwoven basket made by old ladies in Okinawa hangs from the bedroom wall. The small Alvar Aalto Chair65 is the perfect size to place a lamp. We conducted the interview on the eve of the Tanabata Star Festival, so the lamp was decorated with bamboo leaves and the children's wishes written on strips of paper.

3. There are two children's rooms in the home. The kids are free to go back and forth between the two rooms.

4. On top of the staircase is Ishibashi's son's room. While he studies at his desk, his sister reads in the hammock or plays with dolls. The open ceiling, allowing the sounds from the kitchen and living room to filter in, provides a sense of comfort and closeness.

274

Tatsunori Saito
Mayu Saito
Meguro, Tokyo

"My wife and I have similar taste, so we can talk forever about clothes," says Saito. Their shared closet brims over with American casual clothing that they adore. Most of the shoes in the shoe closet near the front entrance, on the other hand, belong to him.

276

While the rest of the world may be on a decluttering craze in pursuit of the simple life, the Saito couple pays it no mind. They delight in collecting as many clothes, shoes, and accessories as they want and filling their life with them without hesitation. The two never tire of discussing fashion, movies, and the books that they love beyond measure. Much like the BEAMS store, entering their apartment is like opening a treasure box, one that makes you feel exhilarated just by looking through it.

Why did you choose to live in this area?
It's close to Shibuya.

What is the theme or rule for your home?
What you see is a natural accumulation of things we love, so there is no particular rule.

What is the most cherished item in your home?
Small items that we just happen to encounter in thrift stores and antique shops.

Do you have any collections or things you can't resist buying?
Denim, bandana, antique items, flannel shirts, and sweatshirts.

Do you have a favorite interior design brand or store?
Search Light in Higashi Shinsaibashi and Indigena in Kita Horie.

Do you have any advice for people who have trouble keeping a tidy home?
Always fold your clothes!

What kind of fashion style do you like?
I like to put together what I like in a way that feels like me.

Which item of clothing do you find most useful when coordinating your everyday style?
Jeans.

Which fashion brands do you prefer when creating your own sense of style?
I don't hesitate buying clothes that appeal to me.

What do you hope to purchase next?
Antique bench and an antique military watch.

How do you hone your sense of style?
See, touch, buy, and wear.

How did you begin working for BEAMS?
I always thought that BEAMS defined American casual. I couldn't get enough of BEAMS BOY either.

What's the best thing about working for BEAMS?
My encounters with people.

1. Many of the small accessories around the kitchen reflect the couple's love for American goods.

2. The couple has a habit of collecting miscellaneous goods like pin badges from thrift stores.

3. Cheerful light shines through the large kitchen window, bouncing off the Fire- King mugs.

4. The patches that decorate the walls are part of a collection. An assortment of Native American jewelry that the couple shares. They always attend the sales event at BEAMS together.

5. Tatsunori is a shoe fanatic and buys at least two pairs a month. The weathered boxes and the random piles of sneakers are part of the interior décor.

6. Bandanas, another of the couple's shared passion, are organized and arranged as you would see in stores. The pin badges on the upper right have the motifs of past American presidents.

7. There are two copies of the same book because they each owned the same book before getting married. A testament to the couple's strong bond.

280

Kazunari Takahashi
Matsudo, Chiba

A mischievous little boy running around, two dogs, and over a hundred cacti. The room flourishes with so many different life forms that it's easy to forget we are in an apartment room. Takahashi's hobby is surfing, and he's skilled enough to have a sponsor. "I'm out in the ocean most weekends. I know so many people associated with the sea, like the local old men." Filled with a calm, laid-back atmosphere, Takahashi's home feels perfectly suited for the beachside sunshine.

What is the most important theme of your lifestyle?
To live where I can feel the sea and nature. Being with my family by the ocean.

Why did you choose to live in this area?
Feeling? Timing? We ended up here somehow.

How do you alleviate stress?
Go to the sea and surf.

What is the theme or rule for your home?
Incorporate surfing and street culture. Keep it as colorful as possible. Add plants for a soothing effect.

What is the most cherished item in your home?
My son's toys.

Do you have any advice for people who have trouble keeping a tidy home?
Try not to let things accumulate and tidy often.

What kind of fashion style do you like?
Surf, Skate, My Style.

Which item of clothing do you find most useful when coordinating your everyday style?
T-shirts, Converse All-Stars.

Which fashion brands do you prefer when creating your own sense of style?
Levi's.

What do you hope to purchase next?
A garage.

How do you hone your sense of style?
By always having an ideal vision.

How did you begin working for BEAMS?
I wanted to be popular with women.

What's the best thing about working for BEAMS?
I became popular with women.

What was the most memorable episode you've had at work?
Meeting my life partner, my wife.

1. & 5. The cacti arranged in the living room and along the veranda of the wooden deck also showcase the work of Takahashi's wife. She grows the cacti acquired at Kasugai city, Aichi prefecture, known for being the number-one grower of cacti in Japan, and sells them through Figueroa, an online shop she established. A carefully curated selection of mugs featuring pop designs.

2. Even the rug has a West Coast vibe.

3. Takahashi's son, always running around, is best friends with the family's dogs.

4. Next to the surfing magazines is a collection of cacti sitting in cups with funny, laid-back designs.

6. Their beloved American Pit Bull Terrier and French Bulldog. Takahashi and his wife are wearing T-shirts with names of surfers and famous beaches by Evenflow. Takahashi provides consultation for the brand at times.

7. Surfboards are a perfect fit for Takahashi's living room, which he wanted to look like "those rooms you see on the West Coast where it's hard to tell if it's a living room or a garage." The unsightly air conditioner system is covered with bandanas and the Stars and Stripes, while his wife's handmade garland adds a further American flair.

THE ENDLESS SUMMER

IN SEARCH OF THE PERFECT WAVE

The poster on the side of the
kitchen counter makes a subtle
nod to the seminal 1966 surfing
documentary, *The Endless
Summer.*

286

Ryohei Onda
Inashiki, Ibaraki

When Onda transferred from the BEAMS shop in Saitama, his colleagues presented him with this rubber tree. Measuring around 10cm at first, the tree grew to nearly one meter tall in seven years and Onda has been hooked on plants ever since. He looks forward to it growing so tall that he won't be able to keep it indoors.

288

With cut flowers, cacti, herbs, succulents, carnivorous plants, and countless other forms of plant life, the Onda residence is a veritable botanical garden. The atmosphere in his room is perpetually changing since he likes to rearrange his furniture to match the condition of his plants, whether they are in bloom or reacting to the weather. "It delights me to watch a tiny bud grow bigger and blossom," Okuda muses, his singular passion for horticulture apparent. He lives among things he holds most dear, and each day feels more precious than the last.

What is the most important theme of your lifestyle?
My family and my plants.

How do you like to spend your day off?
Care for my plants first thing in the morning → Change the water for my cut flowers → Enjoy a meal with family → Go plant hunting → Purchase flowers → Enjoy a meal with family → Go to bed early.

Why did you choose to live in this area?
The breeze and the light here felt great, and I felt from the residences and gardens of other families that we would be able to enjoy a homey relationship with our neighbors.

Do you prefer to rent or buy?
I prefer to buy. My dream is to renovate an old, traditional Japanese-style home. I'd like to grow old with my dream!

How do you alleviate stress?
I'm not the type to get stressed easily, but I do like to rearrange my furniture to refresh my mind.

What is the theme or rule for your home?
The living room is jungle-meets-antiques while the closet is shabby-meets-chinoiserie—I like to change the atmosphere and make sure there's something striking about each room. (Because of my job I feel it's better to invigorate my sensibility this way instead of having every room feel calm and settled.)

What is your favorite spot in your home and how do you like to spend time there?
There are many places but, in the end, wherever my family is laughing together in that moment is my favorite.

Do you have any collections or things you can't resist buying?
I'm always tempted to buy antiques, vintage items, and anything with history that you encounter at flea markets and the like.

Which is your favorite plant?
The kumquat tree I received to commemorate the birth of my daughter.

What kind of fashion style do you like?
I like the "make your own rules" style of the Harajuku streets!

What is your source of information for interior design and fashion?
Instagram! I especially like to check the accounts of flower shops!

How do you hone your sense of style?
The first step is to learn to like yourself. The rest depends on the amount of information you have.

What's the best thing about working for BEAMS?
Being able to cultivate my lifestyle alongside my customers. The brand taught me the value of loving your daily life!

What was the most memorable episode you've had at work?
I came in first in the storewide customer survey twice in a row in 2013 and 2014. If someone like me can become number one, I believe that all sorts of number-one potential lies within so many people! Knowing that makes me so happy!

1

3

4

2

5

1. Staircase decorated with photos of cherished memories of Onda and his wife.

2. Sunglasses belonging to Onda's wife are beautifully displayed.

3. "I'm caring for them every spare moment I get," Onda says. Even on weekends, he gets up early to tend to his garden and water his plants.

4. His beloved daughter, born this year. The new addition is the reason behind the family's perpetual happiness.

5. Flowerpots and vases, purchased at antique shops and flea markets, are selected with emphasis on design rather than functionality. Even dishware is used as flowerpots.

6. The living room, where plants and antiques harmonize, feels comforting. The one-of-a-kind sofa is a beloved relic from Onda's birth home.

7. "I even buy women's accessories as long as the design appeals to me. I especially like pearls, since they feel so feminine," Onda says.

8. A friend who owns a flower shop often delivers fresh plants to the home. The flowers are arranged immediately upon delivery.

6

7 8

292

Hajime Nakajima
Naka, Kanagawa

"My home can be a farm, a house, even the ocean at night. There's nothing better than spending time with friends here, talking about the future of Oiso," says Nakajima. Nakajima is actively engaged in promoting Oiso, his town. He is a proud member of Oiso Farm, a collective that aspires toward a sustainable lifestyle, and he also organizes local food and music events that deliver seasonal, locally sourced food from Oiso. His lifestyle, rooted firmly in the land he loves most, fulfills his heart.

What's your hobby?
Farming and cultivating the fields, playing with music, dyeing cloth.

Do you have any collection or things you can't resist buying?
Band T-shirts.

What's your storage rule?
Inspiration.

What is the most important theme of your lifestyle?
Always be curious and enjoy myself.

What is the theme or rule for your home?
I want to create a room that makes you forget the time.

Do you have a favorite interior design brand or store?
I look at the thing itself instead of the brand. So, when I go shopping, I just let my curiosity guide me into a store.

What kind of fashion style do you like?
I like clothes with interesting colors and styles that allow me to be who I am.

What is your source of information for interior design and fashion?
Spectator, *Brutus*, old books.

What do you hope to purchase next?
Beer-brewing kit.

How do you hone your sense of style?
Take yourself to different places and observe nature and cities.

How did you begin working for BEAMS?
An older colleague of mine introduced me to BEAMS, and I felt that the company values your individuality and character.

What's the best thing about working for BEAMS?
It allows me to meet and collaborate with people working in a wide array of genres.

293

Captions for page 294:
1. Nakajima built the barn with fellow Oiso Farm members, based on the philosophy to "create from zero" as much as possible. From the mud walls to the *sugidama*, or cedar ball, every process has been undertaken by hand. An original logo and pattern of their own brewery are drawn on the mud wall. The cedar ball is a traditional symbol of sake breweries.
2. Nakajima harvests soy beans and makes brewery rice from malted rice, which in turn can be used to make homemade miso.
3. A handmade oven built in the wilderness. "After working up a sweat tilling the land, there's nothing like the taste of freshly cooked rice and sake prepared by friends."
4. A wooden deck built on a high hill offers a panoramic view of the Oiso Farm.

5. The vast scenery as seen from the wooden deck. "There's a hammock here, so if you get tired from farming you can take a nap." Nakajima and the other members are currently developing the second field of the Oiso Farm.

6. The large veranda outside Nakajima's home comes equipped with a convenient sink.

7. A flyer for Oiso Cuppin, a music and food event that Nakajima hosts. For each festival, he chooses a specific country and presents music and food inspired by the

area using local ingredients from Oiso. A free magazine distributed in the Shonan region, which features a column about Oiso Farm.

8. Nakajima has always loved music and dedicates a section of his room to his music.

9. "I'd love to bring more musical culture to Oiso," says Nakajima as he strums a bright rhythm on his cherished guitar. Time in Oiso always seem to pass gently.

An impressive Japanese-style home rooted in tradition. When we step up from the earthen floor, an open space devoid of partitions stretches before us, allowing a refreshing breeze to pass through. The expansive tatami floor beckons us to stretch out, and it's easy to see why the room is a natural gathering spot for friends both young and old. The walls and shelves, fashioned by Gondo's husband, stand alongside interior decors and accessories that Gondo describes as "a simple accumulation of the respective things we like." The home brims with the character and warmth of the husband and wife.

What is the most important theme of your lifestyle?
Nothing really, but we like to display things we like and the work of friends who like to make things.

What is the most cherished item in your home?
The *shimenawa* rope used for purification. I'd like to add a new one every year going forward.

Do you have any collections or things you can't resist buying?
Dishware and handmade washi boxes by Keijusha.

Do you have a favorite interior design brand or store?
Fukugido in Kobe.

Do you have any advice for people who have trouble keeping a tidy home?
Create storage that you can show off.

Which item of clothing do you find most useful when coordinating your everyday style?
Bracelets. I'm in trouble without them.

Which fashion brands do you prefer when creating your own sense of style?
Maria Rudman.

What is your source of information for interior design and fashion?
I always look at *& Premium*.

What do you hope to purchase next?
Shimenawa rope and a big ceramic pot.

How do you hone your sense of style?
No matter the genre, see, touch, and use many "quality things." It's important to make mistakes too.

(Opposite page, top) The room where the couple likes to catch up with each other deftly weaves together Eastern and Scandinavian influences such as a specially ordered, U.K.-exclusive stool by Artek and cushions by Johanna Gullichsen. An illustrated artwork by a friend is displayed in the tokonoma alcove.

1. Right now, *shimenawa* ropes have captured Gondo's heart and won't let go. We spot one as soon as we walk through the front door. The shelf below it doubles as a gallery for seasonal accessories.

2. In an expert display of Eastern and Western influences, Japanese washi lantern is placed on top of the Artek stool, a U.K.-exclusive model.

3. Gondo's husband made the large shoe rack for her growing collection. An impressive lineup of her favorite Converse sneakers.

4. The walls, painted by her husband, add a touch of color to the home. There are many shelves here and there that her husband made upon her request.

5. A roomy bedroom with exposed beams. The hammock makes a luxurious, relaxing time possible.

6. The circular window in the entrance is used to its full aesthetic advantage. A Japanese lamp sits atop the Kurashiki Dantsu woven rug. Gondo's favorite boxes by Keijusha are stored beneath the shelf.

7. Dishware and greens are kept inside a basket from Okinawa. The Artek stool, used as a stand, features a limited color made for the 30th anniversary of BEAMS.

5

6 7

The large window draped with bamboo screens lets in plenty of sunshine and the breeze. The couple enjoys the change and character their 60-year-old home acquires every year, highlighting it with subtle potted plants placed along the porch. While the interior of the home is kept simple and natural, small hints of the couple's unique character and sensibility can be found everywhere.

304

Kei Shimada
Yokohama, Kanagawa

Walking up the gently sloping road, we reach Shimada's home at the top of a slightly elevated hill. Her one-bedroom apartment with a dining room and kitchen benefits from a high ceiling typical of a loft, and the space feels airy and spacious. A pair of Vans Half Cab signed by the legendary skateboarder Steve Caballero hangs from the curtain rail. A prized collection of skateboard decks adorns the wall. The mellow vibe evoked by the scent of freshly ground coffee makes an interesting contrast to the street culture represented in the room, which is best described as a secret hideout.

What is the most important theme of your lifestyle?
Skateboarding.

What is the theme or rule for your home?
Skateboarding and street culture.

What is the most cherished item in your home?
A handmade "skateboarding Daruma" that my colleague gave me when I was transferred at work. It's literally a Daruma that's skateboarding, but its motif is based on an illustration by Jim Phillips, my favorite art director from Santa Cruz. It's a one-of-a-kind item that also has the Japanese kanji character that means "movement," which just so happens to be the word of the year.

Do you have any collection or things you can't resist buying?
Skateboarding accessories.

Do you have any advice for people who have trouble keeping a tidy home?
Throw out what you don't need.

What kind of fashion style do you like?
Skate, surf, work.

Which item of clothing do you find most useful when coordinating your everyday style?
A pair of jeans by Mister Freedom, which I've been wearing and loving for about three years. I love the wide, straight fit.

Which fashion brands do you prefer when creating your own sense of style?
Toyo Enterprise, Kaptain Sunshine, Battenwear.

What is your source of information for interior design and fashion?
Instagram account of foreign skateboarding shops. Jokers Skate Shop in L.A. and Skate City Supply in New Mexico, for example.

How do you hone your sense of style?
Pursue what you like.

306

(Opposite page) Shimada enjoys freshly ground coffee in a pool of light streaming through the window. Today's Ethiopian coffee beans were purchased at Pretty Things near Komazawa University.

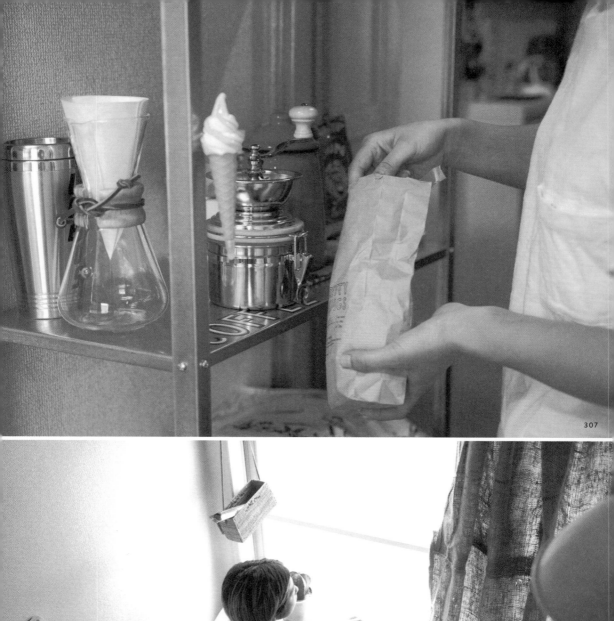

1. Colorful magnets gathered from trips to locations overseas such as New Mexico and California.

2. A display of rare skateboard decks: Lurkville, a skateboard deck company that got its start in San Diego; Santa Cruz featuring a grownup "Mad Dog"; Evil Good displaying the iconic shape of the state of California.

3. Vans shoe boxes complement the vibe of the room perfectly.

4. The light blue cupboard is by Ikea. We glimpsed a few pieces of pottery from Moyai Kogei in Kamakura.

5. Essential and stylish items for coffee break: Bright red enamel pot; stainless steel mill; the Chemex coffee maker was a birthday gift.

6. A handmade table inspired by the coffee table featured in the film, *Coffee and Cigarettes*. The ingenious piece also doubles as a kotatsu heater.

7. Sneaker collection. The shoe boxes are kept organized and used as presentable storage.

8. The front door, decorated with flyers, is reminiscent of an American garage.

310

Mayumi Inoue
Nagareyama, Chiba

Climbing up the staircase decorated with wooden objects in a bevy of shapes and sizes in the manner of a mini art gallery, Inoue lead us into her living room. Once inside, the colorful patterns immediately rush into view. The organic and stirring pictures drawn by her artist husband harmonize just so with the wooden furniture and plants, creating a rhythm to the space. Suffused with a natural and bright mood, the room brims with energy.

What is the most important theme of your lifestyle?
To surround myself with plants and pictures.

What is the theme or rule for your home?
Nature and art.

What is the most cherished item in your home?
My husband's artwork.

Do you have any collections or things you can't resist buying?
Plants and antique accessories.

Do you have a favorite interior design brand or store?
I often buy antique accessories from my friend's shop, Humming Bird.

Which item of clothing do you find most useful when coordinating your everyday style?
Accessories made by artists that I purchased at the market. Handmade necklaces I received from younger colleagues and customers at work.

How do you hone your sense of style?
Meet and talk with many people. Be with people who inspire you.

How did you begin working for BEAMS?
I gained experience by working in sales for two years for a different apparel company. Then I joined BEAMS, which I've always liked.

What was the most memorable episode you've had at work?
When a customer who frequents the store came in carrying a bag my husband made. When I asked her how she got it, she told me that she's always liked the artist's work and that she had just purchased it. When I told her my husband made it, she was so shocked. I felt a magical sense of fate.

311

Inoue's husband adds a new hue to his work in progress. Inoue holds a wooden Daruma from See See. "I purchased it at BEAMS Planets and had my husband paint it." The customized, one-of-a-kind piece is now her beloved treasure.

1. A decorative pillow on the sofa has been customized with Inoue's husband's characteristic "checkered" pattern.

2. A series of portraits of friends drawn in warm, unique colors.

3. Paint tubes hang neatly from racks.

4. Inoue's favorite plant, kept inside an antique textile bag with handles, is looped around a tree branch with a gentle, naturally curving form. Illustrations are accented by wooden frames.

5. Her husband's art supplies and a palette featuring an array of colors he uses.

6. Artwork is found everywhere in the room. "My favorite piece is my portrait," Inoue says. Awash in vivid yellow and set against a well-worn wooden frame, the portrait makes a striking presence in the room.

7. Plants, which Inoue likes to purchase at Moora Moora, a shop near Kashiwa station. The pots and vases, painted in vibrant colors, brighten the space even more.

316

Hiroshi Kondo
Kamakura, Kanagawa

Across from Kondo's home runs a small river where fireflies still dance in the summer, a rare sign of untamed nature. His home sits atop a steep stone staircase, where a plum tree welcomes visitors into the garden. "I'm comforted when I know that the things in my home have been previously owned by someone," says Kondo, who lives in a renovated fifty-year-old home. The benefit of a traditional Japanese-style home is that the veranda remains warm while the interior of the house stays cool even during the summer. Kondo's daily morning routine includes watering his plants and caring for his killifish, while keeping an eye out for the birds and squirrels that visit his garden. Being among nature and old things is Kondo's way of life.

What's your hobby?
Gardening, collecting outdoor gear, and interior décor.

Do you have any collections or things you can't resist buying?
Old books.

What's your storage rule?
I group things by color, shape, and genre. I try to keep the quantity of the things I own to an optimum amount.

What is the most important theme of your lifestyle?
To live where you can feel nature (and the countryside).

What is the theme or rule for your home?
I like to collect things with eclectic tastes (industrial, Scandinavian, and retro pieces from the Showa period) regardless of genre.

What is your favorite spot in your home and how do you like to spend time there?
I like to relax in my living room with its high ceiling and exposed beams.

Why did you choose to live in this area?
I was born and raised here in Kanagawa. I also like the nature.

What kind of fashion style do you like?
Standard thrift clothes that have become the foundation of men's wear. I also like to combine basic clothes with items that have playful designs.

Which item of clothing do you find most useful when coordinating your everyday style?
Hats.

What do you hope to purchase next?
Antique glass from the Showa period.

How do you hone your sense of style?
Always be interested and curious. Even if something is a little out of your budget, buy it and make it your own. Learn from the experience of owning something.

What's the best thing about working for BEAMS?
Having countless number of colleagues with a strong sense of identity (and integrity).

Captions for page 320:
1. & 3. Colorful glasses purchased in Okinawa. The natural coloring of Scandinavian tableware from Rorstrand and Arabia blend seamlessly into the atmosphere. The illustrated dish by Arabia doubles as a sweet decorative object.
2. A space for Kondo's hobbies, such as mountain climbing gear. He got hooked on mountain climbing ever since he went hiking in his twenties with Mr. Hirosawa, a famed buyer at BEAMS who has earned the nickname "God of Mountains" by his colleagues. After Kondo moved to Kamakura, hiking the nearby Kinubariyama, with its impressive view of the ocean, became part of his routine.

It's only been a month and a half since Kondo moved to this fifty-year-old traditional Japanese home, whose interior he has spent half a year renovating. The antique door along the porch—korado in Japanese—is from the Taisho era, and he even replaced the shoji screens with an antique find from the Showa era. Antiques in an old traditional home—the layers upon layers of history exhume a sense of nostalgia.

4. Vintage copies of *The Whole Earth Catalog* and *Made in USA* from the '60s and '70s sit among his books on mountain climbing and plants.

5. *Alp*, a booklet about mountains published in the early Showa period. Kondo fell in love with the cover.

6. An exposed fluorescent lamp and an industrial lamp made in France in the '60s illuminate Kondo's large stainless-steel kitchen. Industrial furniture and the old, Japanese-style home make an inspired combination.

7. Various succulents and cacti also featured in *BEAMS AT HOME Vol. 2*. Since the plants had been largely kept indoors before Kondo moved to his house, it's taking them a while to adjust to their new outdoor spot.

8. Doors and glass windows that existed before Kondo renovated the house are scattered throughout. Kondo handpicked this antique door, known as Kurado in Japanese.

6

8

321

322

Shinsuke Nakada
Junko Nakada
Kamakura, Kanagawa

We find the home in a quiet residential district a short distance from Kamakura station. "The theme for my home is to live simply and with ease," says Nakada. Nakada's home is modeled after the Eames House, a masterpiece of modern architecture built in the United States in 1949. The home has a square exterior and its living room, a space constructed with minimal, linear lines and populated with treasured furniture and plants, is an epitome of comfort. Located at an ideal distance from the city, the house also makes marking a clear boundary between work and personal life easy. Surrounded by his family and passion, Nakada enjoys his life in Kamakura to the fullest.

What is the most important theme of your lifestyle?
A sense of playfulness. I'm always thinking about how I can add more joy to my life.

Do you prefer to rent or buy?
I prefer to buy. Getting a mortgage ignites the fuse of your life.

What is the most important way to spend your time?
Imagine, simulate, examine, and reflect. I place great value in thinking about things.

Do you have any collections or things you can't resist buying?
Commodities and mass-produced vintage products that have survived the test of time to this contemporary era

without breaking down. I'm always tempted to reach for mass-produced goods with a formal beauty, even if they were considered cheap back in the day.

Do you have a favorite interior design brand or store?
I love all American antique shops. I have fun searching for things and it feels like an opportunity to utilize what I have learned and studied. You can only discover things once in a lifetime, after all.

What kind of fashion style do you like?
I like American casual style with details and functions that have a history to them.

What do you hope to purchase next?
A bicycle from Alex Moulton.

How do you hone your sense of style?
Nurture your motivation to absorb things.

How did you begin working for BEAMS?
Even when I was a student, I could not imagine working for any company other than BEAMS. I was attracted to BEAMS because it has an unwavering core no matter what dizzying changes the fashion business is going through, yet it also has the ability to remain flexible and one step ahead.

What's the best thing about working for BEAMS?
I'm just incredibly blessed when it comes to relationships with people. This fact alone is my greatest fortune.

What was the most memorable episode you've had at work?
Being able to work with L.L. Bean. We dedicated a lot of time to building a trusting relationship with them, and I'll never forget how moved I was to collaborate with the pioneer of outdoor brands.

On the wall flanked by two large windows is a work by Nakada's beloved photographer, Gentaro Ishizuka. The windows offer changing views of the mountains through the four seasons.

WHAT
GOOD SHALL
I DO THIS
DAY?

1. From the window, you can see colorful flags hanging from the tree in the mountain behind the house. Nakada attached the flags himself.

2. The striking wooden ladder was purchased at Jantiques in Nakameguro. Back when Nakada was living in Tokyo, he used to make the rounds in the furniture store district near Gakugei-daigaku Station.

3. A message plate with the words, "WHAT GOOD SHALL I DO THIS DAY?" is from the New York outdoor brand, Best Made. Nakada affixed the plate at the bottom of the staircase and always looks at it before heading out to work.

4. The stainless-steel countertop and other details in the light-filled, open kitchen are also molded after the Eames House.

5. Nakada used to go to New Mexico often when he was a buyer. The rugs in the living room are by Centinela, a brand he's been working with for a long time.

6. The doors to the bathroom and the first-floor children's room were painted in a color that complement the white wall.

7. Pieces by beloved artists, including Ryoji Homma, Koji Toyoda, and Matt Katayama, adorn the child's room.

5

227

6

7

328

🏠 🚺 | Risa Sawada
Bunkyo, Tokyo

329

Sawada's home has been converted from a traditional Japanese-style house built forty years ago in the *shitamachi* district or old downtown, an area still reminiscent of Tokyo's good old days. In her home, her beloved cat, Kotora, roams freely. "I'm not very particular. As long as the atmosphere of the home is comfortable for me and my cat, I'm happy." With the help of an interior decorator she knows as well as close friends, Sawada patiently built her DIY home piece by piece. Sawada lives with an affinity for quality, time-honored items that should be passed down through the generations, a lifestyle that's all the more important in this contemporary era.

What is the most important theme of your lifestyle?
To live truthfully to my heart without unnecessary strain.

Why did you choose to live in this area?
A friend introduced me to the area. I wanted to be soothed by the warm human connection characteristic of *shitamachi* and the quiet energy of the Nezu Shrine.

How do you alleviate stress?
Laugh. Move your body. Interact with nature. Drink and enjoy sake.

What is the most cherished item in your home?
My guest bed, discovered in a mansion belonging to a friend's grandfather, cannot be found anywhere else. It also doubles as a sofa so I want to take good care of it.

Do you have a favorite interior design brand or store?
It's hard to narrow down to just one, but I have absolute faith in Fennica, which is where I worked originally.

What kind of fashion style do you like?
Nothing that looks like you are trying too hard. Something simple that you don't easily tire of, a style that's comfortable and easy to move in.

What do you hope to purchase next?
A longboard, a car, a new MacBook, a huge cushion.

How do you hone your sense of style?
Go to many different places, see everything, and talk to people. Do not set a boundary around your world.

How did you begin working for BEAMS?
When I was interviewing for jobs, I chose BEAMS because I was able to have the most fun and be myself.

What was the most memorable episode you've had at work?
When BEAMS TAIPEI, which I worked on from the ground up, finally opened.

331

Used as a sofa is an old guest bed, a gift from the grandfather of Sawada's German friend. It's weathered just so, making it all the more comforting. The cushion covers were stitched from vintage Marimekko and Artek cloths.

1. Fish mobile made of Japanese washi paper was purchased at Isetatsu in the Yanaka district. It hangs and sways by the windowsill in the living room.

2. Sawada's home is cleverly designed so that her cat, Kotora, can climb and play. The cat food dish is by Alessi.

3. The hanging washi paper lantern, a present from a friend's grandfather, and fruits of wild red rose set an elegant mood.

4. The handmade detachable shelf with a stuffed frog decorated with a pin that reads, "Kiss me I'm a prince." "Here I display things that I've always liked and kept since I was

little," Sawada muses. "The balls are actually made of Kotora's fur. It turned out this way when I was rolling it around in my hands."

5. The plants in the room are arrangements by 198 Queen St. Kingston in Sendagi. The boldly planted green spruces up the dining room table.

6. A coat of cobalt blue paint enlivens the second-floor bedroom. A showcase of memorable photographs.

7. A refreshing breeze blows through the open window, filling the room with a positive energy.

Sawada and Kotora relax on the canvas Nychair X. Kotora, now twelve, has been with her since he was a kitten. Sawada is like a mom to Kotora and they are inseparable at home. The purple vintage linen draped over the chair harmonizes the gentle atmosphere of the room.

334

Yoshinori Sato
Nami Sato
Setagaya, Tokyo

Folk crafts fashioned by people who represent their home—Akita and Okinawa prefectures—blend into the life of husband and wife who both grew up in the countryside, surrounded by nature. Such folk crafts are both efficient and functional; they are immune to the whims of trends and shine with a true "beauty of utility." If a home is indeed a reflection of its residents, then the serene presence and the warm, welcoming air of the couple are echoed by the items in their home. No matter where they come from, these items can harmonize with their surroundings, nestling close to one's life for a long time.

What is the most important theme of your lifestyle?
To stay conscious of our overall health. (Be a little bit particular about the quality of our food, exercise, and sleep.)

What is the most important way to spend your time?
I value my "off" time from the moment I come home from work to when I go to sleep.

What is the theme or rule for your home?
To organize by area, country, or era.

What is the most cherished item in your home?
Pirkka table by Ilmari Tapiovaara and the ceremonial Songye mask, which was a gift from an older colleague.

Do you have any collections or things you can't resist buying?
Plants and masks. *Shirayuki-fukin*, which are Japanese dishcloths. The word translates to, "snow white towels."

Do you have a favorite interior design brand or store?
Rungta in Kyodo and Fridge in Kamimachi.

Do you have any advice for people who have trouble keeping a tidy home?
Display all the things you like. The things you could not display are things you don't need.

Which item of clothing do you find most useful when coordinating your everyday style?
T-shirts with pockets and shorts. Below-the-knee skirts.

What is your source of information for interior design and fashion?
Transit and *dia Standard*.

How do you hone your sense of style?
Purchase things and hang out with many different people. Challenge yourself and have conversations with many people.

How did you begin working for BEAMS?
Whenever I used to go into the store as a customer, I felt so euphoric as if I were on a treasure hunt because BEAMS was a store where I could always find something I wanted. I began working for the brand because I knew that the store has the ability to delight anyone who comes in contact with it, not just myself.

What's the best thing about working for BEAMS?
I feel inspired and have so much fun everyday. I'm also able to take part in launching a variety of stores. I think if I include the times I've visited outside of work, I've been to almost every BEAMS store in the country.

On the decorative shelf in the dining room are folk crafts representing the respective homes of the husband and wife: Sato is from Akita prefecture and his wife is a native of Okinawa prefecture. Folk crafts from around the world, including a Scandinavian Dansk bowl in which a collection of bandanas is kept, are also among the eclectic display.

337

1. A wedding welcome sign in India ink, a gift made by an older co-worker at BEAMS.

2. Yoshinori's favorite Indian jewelry. He selected most of the interior décor of the room, a mixture of multi-national folk crafts, to suit his taste.

3. *Shirayuki-fukin*, the Japanese dishcloths that Nami likes to collect, were all purchased at BEAMS. "They're so easy to use and there are so many colors and patterns that I can't help collecting them," she explains.

4. Storing air plants and dried flowers in a basket from Akita prefecture is a simple yet enviable idea.

5. Dried ears of Peruvian corn make an excellent match for the modern African cloth.

6. Displayed on top of the cabinet in the living room is a ceremonial Songye mask, which Yoshinori got from an older co-worker.

7. "There is no greater bliss than a time to read leisurely," Yoshinori says. A pile of his books in a section of the living room.

8. A subtle presentation of folk crafts on the dining room table. "I always want to feel Okinawa, which I love, even when I'm home, so folk crafts from the prefecture tend to accumulate," Nami says.

6 339

8

340

Takashi Kano
Oita City, Oita

The overflowing greenery outside the window immediately capture our attention as we step into Kano's living room. But he has no backyard or fertile land to speak of. "You can grow orchids without soil," Kano explains, showing us the orchids that grow on fragments of wood and cork. For Kano, his home exists for his plants. He spares no creative solution or effort in raising his plants, and he grows ever fonder of them the more he cares for them. His veranda, from where he can survey the city of Oita below, is small but thriving with life.

What is the most important theme of your lifestyle?
Eat good food and drink. Live and watch my plants flourish.

Do you prefer to rent or buy?
I rent right now. But I would love to live in a house. I want to build an amazing garden and a greenhouse where I can grow as many orchids as I like.

What is the most important way to spend your time?
Watering my plants every morning. On the weekend, I like to eat dinner early, drink, and relax at home.

What is your favorite spot in your home and how do you like to spend time there?
I like watering my flowers on the veranda. I like to spend time tending to their roots and seedlings.

What is the most cherished item in your home?
The dining table by Ilmari Tapiovaara and the Wishbone Chair by Hans Wegner.

Do you have any collections or things you can't resist buying?
Orchids, plants, bowls, and folk toys (especially papier-mâché).

Do you have a favorite interior design brand or store?
In Fukuoka I like Foucault, Placerworkshop, Standard Manual, and Bouun. Also, Spica in Oita.

What kind of fashion style do you like?
In general, I like outdoor clothes. I also gravitate toward white and black, monochromatic ensembles.

What do you hope to purchase next?
Old Kilims, Akari by Isamu Noguchi (one that looks like horns), and a Helinox cot.

How do you hone your sense of style?
See and learn from great things. If you think something is great, don't be afraid to dive in head first. Study hard. Listen carefully to other people.

How did you begin working for BEAMS?
When I was a student I loved thrift stores and wanted to work for an apparel company. An employee at a thrift store I used to frequent told me, "You'll learn more if you work for a big company." Now that I think about it, that may have been another way of saying they couldn't hire me at that store, but that's how I ended up applying to BEAMS. The person who would later become my boss interviewed me three times, and I really admired him so I decided to join.

What's the best thing about working for BEAMS?
I met superiors and bosses I respect, colleagues who inspire me, and younger co-workers I can trust.

344

1. Not even the small corners of the kitchen are without a hint of green. Warabi baskets from Okinawa are used to camouflage planters.
2. Papier-mâché figurines that Kano cannot resist collecting adorn the cupboard.
3. Mud-dyed cloth by the Dogon peoples of Mali on display in the living room, which offers a panoramic view of Kano's plants.
4. Kano likes to drink while reading about plants and bowls. His favorite is *The Illustrated Guide of Orchids*.

5. Various folk crafts fit right into the atmosphere of Kano's home. A balancing toy he fell in love with in a store in Tokyo floats soothingly.
6. Stools of varying colors, shapes, and materials line the wall that extends from the kitchen to the living room. The stools are useful in a number of ways, from sitting to decorating with plants and other objects.
7. An Oaxacan wood carving in a bamboo basket by Jurgen Lehl; African raffia and a Baule chair. Folk crafts from around the world blend into the scene.

345

346

■ | 👪 | Hitomi Hashimoto
Nara City, Nara

Simple fabrics, cute baubles, and plants inhabit the warm, wooden interior. Plants and artwork by Lisa Larson welcoming you at the entrance set the gentle tone in the Hashimoto residence. Her son plays with car toys, using the pattern on the rug by Woodnotes as a road. Hashimoto and her husband look on, a picture of an ideal family amidst a home inspired by Scandinavia.

What is your theme or rule for interior design?
I love wooden objects, Scandinavian design, and folk crafts, so I try to make those the foundation of my interior décor. It's always my goal to keep things tidy and simple though.

Do you have a favorite interior design brand or store?
Timeless in Shukugawa.

Do you have any advice for people who have trouble keeping a tidy home?
Enjoy tidying. Set a time line and tidy one location per day. And just be happy that you've done something!

What kind of fashion style do you like?
I prefer basic styles now that I have a child. I particularly love the color navy.

How do you hone your sense of style?
Look at a variety of stores and get inspired. Don't stay cooped up at home. Branch out and talk to many different people, not just those in the same industry as you.

348

1. The bright living and dining room are tied together by Scandinavian influences. In addition to low chairs by Alvar Aalto and Tendo Mokko, there is an Asian chair by 6 [rock], that their son fell in love with. This is the favorite place for the family to hang out.

2. An indigo table runner by Kurashiki Dantsu is spread out on top of the chest, punctuated by a small bowl.

3. On top of the small shelf by the entrance are monkey figurine by Kay Bojesen, wooden accessories, and a single flower pottery vase. On the wall is a silk screen with a serial number created by Rie Ito at Birds' Words. The sweet collection of straw hats belongs to their son.

4. On the veranda are plants and unique, bushy cacti.

5. Toys are considered part of the interior décor. Things that get cluttered easily are kept nice and tidy in baskets.

352

🏢 | 🚺🚹 | Yoko Kanomata
Itabashi, Tokyo

Kanomata, an animal lover, lives together with her partner, a plant lover. True to her wish to co-exist in harmony with living things, her room is populated by unusual plant life and amusing animal accessories. On weekends, Kanomata likes to water her plants on the veranda or flip through her illustrated book of owls while thinking about Edward and Yumil, her two avian friends at the owl café she likes to visit. Hers is a peaceful home watched over by creatures of all kinds.

What's your hobby?
Ever since I transferred to BEAMS Yokohama, I've been researching packable meals for my bento lunch.

Do you have any collection or things you can't resist buying?
Animal trinkets.

What's your storage rule?
I like to store my tableware by displaying them. I love and want to use all of my tableware equally, so I like to store them where I can see them.

What is the theme or rule for your home?
To co-exist with plants, pictures, and living things (even ornaments) in every space.

What is the most cherished item in your home?
The stuffed fabric pigeon I fell in love with at Biotop.

Do you have a favorite interior design brand or store?
A vintage clothes, accessories, and plants store called Sein in Yutenji.

How do you alleviate stress?
I go to the owl café in Ikebukuro three to four times a month. I like to watch over the growth of two birds in particular.

What kind of fashion style do you like?
I like three-dimensional designs such as gathers and frills.

Which fashion brands do you prefer when creating your own sense of style?
RBS.

What do you hope to purchase next?
A wooden stool (for using as a stepladder or resting while cooking).

How do you hone your sense of style?
Interact with more people.

How did you begin working for BEAMS?
I wanted to always surround myself with the stylish clothes and staff at BEAMS so that I can be stylish myself.

What's the best thing about working for BEAMS?
Making connections with people. Since I work for a company I love, I've developed the mental capacity to overcome my weakness and improve.

Kanomata lives with her partner, who was a former staff member at BEAMS. A bicycle, pair of boots, and edgy abstract art welcome guests by the front door. The Red Wing boots miraculously survived when Kanomata's birth home suffered earthquake damage. Masculine sensibility seen throughout the room is counter-balanced by the unexpected sweetness of animal accessories.

1. The vintage Eames chair in the bedroom. A cute stuffed pigeon rests on top.

2. Kanomata has been packing bento lunches to work since the spring. She prepares her meals in advance and packs them carefully every morning.

3. & 4. The collection of artwork in her home belongs to her partner. Most pieces were purchased at Sein, their favorite store. The storeowner buys thrift clothes, plants, and accessories from overseas, and the couple can't help but stay long whenever they visit.

5. The tableware are boldly displayed on the steel shelves. "Since I can see where everything is, the variety of dishes I

use has increased." The bowls were purchased at ceramic markets or trips to the countryside.

6. Kanomata's partner loves plants and has an encyclopedic knowledge of them. The plants hanging in the living room were purchased at Ozaki Flower Park. More plants thrive in the veranda outside. Kanomata chose this apartment specifically for its veranda, which has ample space for growing plants.

7. Kanomata's favorite book. Pictured on the left is the same long-eared owl as Yumil, her favorite owl at the owl café. "I became hooked after my first visit."

8. The military trunk is used as a table in the bedroom. "I added animal accessories to keep it from getting too boyish."

357

358

🏠 | 👨‍👧‍👦 | Hiroshi Kubo
Yokohama, Kanagawa

As a buyer, director of BEAMS BOY, and designer of concert costumes for the aritst Noriyuki Makihara, Hiroshi Kubo has spearheaded many iconic projects for BEAMS. "What I love is the mixture," he says of his residence, a milieu consisting of walls made of diatomaceous earth, baseball goods, a one-of-a-kind cat tree, and surfing items that inspire his innovative ideas. A physical embodiment of BEAMS itself, Kubo's home is where he can feel most like himself.

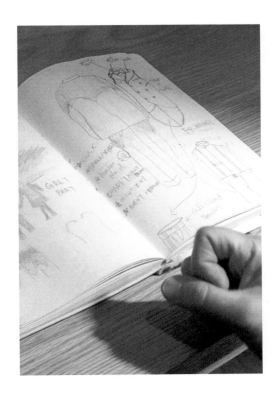

What is the most important theme of your lifestyle?
To have a lounge-like space where I can spend a comfortable time with my cat.

What is the theme or rule for your home?
I mixed in my own way the atmosphere and things that I like or find appealing across a variety of genres—everything that I cultivated during the last thirty years at BEAMS—and incorporated them to create an original style. I asked Hiroto Aranishi, the furniture designer of 6[rock], to create a one-of-a-kind cat tree, and my idea was to make that into a focal point of the room.

What is the most cherished item in your home?
Natural wood furniture, including my dining room table, coffee table in the lounge, work desk, and the cat tower made by Aranishi-san, mentioned above.

Do you have a favorite interior design brand or store?
Fennica within International Gallery BEAMS; Schoolhouse Electric & Co. in Portland; Truck Furniture; Aranishi-san's workshop, 6[rock].

What kind of fashion style do you like?
My foundation is American traditional, and I like to add a dash of mode or SK8ER elements to it.

How do you hone your sense of style?
I think by owning and experiencing things that interest you or appeal to you as much as possible, it becomes a part of your sensibility. It all comes down to your own experience.

How did you begin working for BEAMS?
One of my sister's friends was a BEAMS employee, and that influenced me to become a fan of BEAMS and I started going to the store all the time. I started working there part-time when I entered university. After graduation I became their full-time employee right away. I was totally head-over-heels for BEAMS.

What's the best thing about working for BEAMS?
I'm surrounded by apparel and products that I love, and I get to introduce them to customers and share that joy with them and the staff.

What was the most memorable episode you've had at work?
Pitching the label BEAMS BOY internally and seeing it come to life. Also, managing to open a BEAMS pop-up store twice at Disney Sea. I'm also proud of having been in charge of the concert tour costumes for the artist Noriyuki Makihara for many years.

A diehard baseball fan, Kubo has countless pieces of merchandise and memorabilia. He currently serves as the director of the project "BAYSTARS with BEAMS," creating various fan gear with high fashion sense.

What immediately catches the eye after we enter the front door is the shoe closet, which occupies a whole room. The vast wall of loafers and sneakers is quite a sight. Kubo says he can't help entering his closet and admiring his collection at least once a day.

1. As soon as we step inside, a soaring lounge welcomes us inside. The light bouncing off the Italian blue walls feels refreshing.
2. Pat Metheny, Kubo's favorite artist. The autographed CD complete with a backstage pass was an unexpected find at Amoeba Music in San Francisco.
3. On the shelf in the lounge we find a skateboard deck by Stereo, founded by Jason Lee and Chris Pastras.

4. Cat tree built by the furniture craftsman Hiroto Aranishi, with whom Kubo has a close relationship, both personally and professionally. Kubo's cat loves to perch on the tower, which benefits from the warm quality of white oak.
5. The lounge is the place where Kubo can feel most at ease. Gazing at his eclectic bookshelf and letting his thoughts flow always help generate new ideas.
6. Kubo's favorite way to spend time: sitting on the Le Corbusier sofa and listening leisurely to music.

364

Akihiro Ozeki
Machida, Tokyo

A lover of the great outdoors, Ozeki built a Mountain Hardwear tent inside his Japanese-style room so he and his kids can sleep inside on the weekends. "Play baseball or go surfing, buy some materials and cook at home, then enjoy a meal as a family. That's the definition of the best weekend for me." On the day of the interview, he treated us to udon noodles that he made from scratch. Warmth and careful attention to detail is seen in every aspect of his family's life.

What is the most important theme of your lifestyle?
Simplicity.

What is your theme or rule for interior design?
I pay attention to balance, design, and the overall color, but when it comes down to it, I just purchase what strikes me as great! I judge the book by its cover.

What is the most cherished item in your home?
A lounge chair from Plycraft.

Do you have a favorite interior design brand or store?
A general store called Bubble Oven, which is built on a parking lot of an American-style diner.

Do you have any advice for people who have trouble keeping a tidy home?
Try not to hoard things.

What kind of fashion style do you like?
A simple style that you can still wear three years from now.

Which fashion brands do you prefer when creating your own sense of style?
Denim, starting with a pair of Levi's.

Are there any magazines, books, or people that inspire your interior design and fashion?
Social media sites abroad such as Instagram, Pinterest, and Fancy.

What do you hope to purchase next?
A set of cookware from All-Clad. A BBQ grill I can place in the backyard.

How do you hone your sense of style?
With the power of information.

What is your personal mantra?
When your heart changes, your action changes; when your action changes, your habits change; when your habits change, your personality changes; when your personality changes, your fate changes.

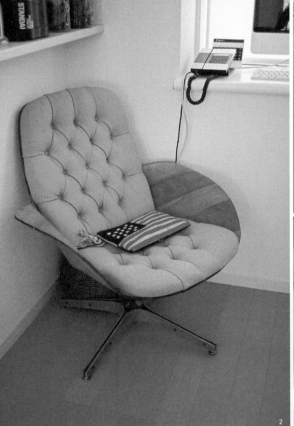

1. Succulents and cacti adorn the windowsill along the staircase. Using cooking utensils and empty cans with eye-catching designs as vases is the Ozeki way.

2. A vintage chair he purchased in Palm Springs, where he went on his first business trip after joining BEAMS. "I liked the chair, but I knew it would cost a fortune transporting it so I almost gave up. That's when our president, Shitara, encouraged me by saying 'Wouldn't it be amazing if a chair you encountered in Palm Springs was in your home?' and he footed half the transportation cost. My colleagues also helped me bring it back all the way to the airport. It's a memorable piece."

3. A patchwork quilt using vintage fabric from Marimekko hangs by the staircase. Ilmari Tapiovaara stools, bracken basket from Okinawa, and drums and African accessories purchased at L.A.'s Rose Bowl Flea Market.

4. The sofa in the living room are all from Tendo Mokko. Alongside the window are single seaters made of leather that gets better with age.

370

Noriko Aoki
Williamsburg, Brooklyn, U.S.A

Williamsburg, the most popular neighborhood in Brooklyn in recent years, is a hub of artists and creatives. Aoki's apartment stands in a quiet corner surrounded by trees. Her beloved dog, August, passed away this spring, but her mementos are still treasured around the home, matching perfectly with Aoki's vintage furniture and folk crafts that she inherited from her parents. Aoki has a knack for presenting a space filled with a gentle and cozy air.

What is the most important theme of your lifestyle?
I don't have a particular theme; my apartment started to look this way naturally as I collected personal things that I love. I like to cherish old things that have a warmth to them. I even buy furniture at garage sales.

What is your theme or rule for interior design?
My style is an eclectic fusion. I like neutral colors, and I like to collect practical items that appeal to me without adhering too much to a specific era or style.

What is the most cherished item in your home?
Relics of August, who passed away this spring, and my antiques and folk craft collection that I inherited from my parents. I have a chest from the Joseon Dynasty and a serving tray made out of a single plate of Japanese zelkova. I treasure them all.

Do you have any collections or things you can't resist buying?
I try not to collect anything, but small accessories of rabbits tend to gather in my home since my friends give them to me.

Do you have a favorite interior design brand or store?
A vintage furniture store called RePOP in Williamsburg. They have so many mid-century modern pieces.

Do you have any advice for people who have trouble keeping a tidy home?
Don't put dirty things around the house. Place everything where it belongs. For instance, don't put kitchen accessories in the bedroom. Be diligent about cleaning often.

What kind of fashion style do you like?
Things that reflect my mood and the weather at the time. I don't like anything that's too formal or overdone, so I like to infuse something that feels a little offbeat. For example, if I'm wearing a dress I'll try to keep what I put on my feet casual.

Which fashion brands do you prefer when creating your own sense of style?
Boy by Band of Outsiders, Engineered Garments, 3.1 Philip Lim, J.Crew.

Are there any magazines, books, or people that inspire your interior design and fashion?
An image I saw somewhere, places I've visited in my travels, and tiny, privately owned stores and restaurants.

How do you hone your sense of style?
I think it's important to look at things that are considered top class or high quality, regardless of whether or not you like them. I also think you can hone your style by going to the theater or seeing art, films, and experiencing fine dining.

What is your personal mantra?
Go with the flow. That's my motto for life.

1. A simple display around the mirror in the living room. The catch-all of a mythical Jackalope, with antlers of a deer and the body of a rabbit, was a gift from a friend.
2. Aoki likes to relax on the sofa, reading magazines and books. Her living room floods with sunlight.

3. A dog cushion by Areaware, modeled after the beloved dog of the fashion photographer Bruce Weber.
4. Aoki is not particular about brands, but her favorite everyday bag is a canvas tote by Hermès. She keeps it looking sweet with a corsage.

375

376

 | | Takafumi Aida
Shoko Aida
Yokohama, Kanagawa

Looking out from the terrace of this apartment room, the lush green trees grow densely in front, and beyond them stretches out the faraway cityscape. As if echoing such a landscape, Aida's home is filled with plants, and African wooden sculptures and Adam Silverman's pottery blend seamlessly inside. Aida remarks that his particularly large cactus makes replanting a hassle, but he and his wife enjoy the time it takes looking for a new pot and taking care of the plant daily. Aida's home gives a warm impression, a place to slow down and savor the day.

What is the most important theme of your lifestyle?
Whenever I need a break, I go fishing, which is something I've enjoyed since I was in middle school. I like to spend my life surrounded by plant life and taking it slow.

Do you have any collection or things you can't resist buying?
Horticulture, fishing goods, *mingei* folkcrafts.

Do you have a favorite interior design brand or store?
Qusamura (plants), Kohaen (plants), Talo (Scandinavian furniture), P.F.S. Parts Center (furniture), Japanese lacquer ware by Osamu Matsuzaki.

Do you have any advice for people who have trouble keeping a tidy home?
Before you purchase anything, try to imagine how you will use it and where you will put it.

What kind of fashion style do you like?
A style that mixes vintage pieces. I like a style that's relaxed and unexpected, like pairing a casual pair of shorts with an elegant knitted top.

Which fashion brands do you prefer when creating your own sense of style?
Ts(s); Patagonia; Engineered Garments; vintage clothes.

Are there any magazines, books, or people that inspire your interior design and fashion?
Saltwater; Kohei Oda of Qusamura.

What do you hope to purchase next?
Plants by Qusamura; works by Osamu Matsuzaki.

How do you hone your sense of style?
Challenge yourself in various ways (sports, outdoor activities).

What is your personal mantra?
Enjoy the process.

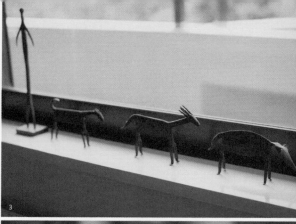

378

1. Aida and his wife Shoko relax with their pet dog, Chico. At the back of the dining space is a collection of the couple's favorite plants. The succulents purchased at Qusamura look beautiful against the white wall. Instead of simply displaying their essential pottery and folk crafts, they actually use them so that they blend into their lifestyle. The Louis Poulsen lighting ever so warmly illuminates their collection of dishware, all infused with the rhythm of the couple's life.

2. Musical scores by legends of the classic music world including Beethoven, Bach, and Chopin line the bookshelf in the corner of the room. Shoko plays the piano from time to time. Listening to her play while relaxing is a treat for her husband as well.

3. Tiny animal and human figurines are arranged on top of the narrow space by the window. The African folk crafts are subtle elements that blend seamlessly into the space. Their small but calming presence catches your eyes at unexpected moments.

4. The couple's well-organized kitchen. Pots and pans, stainless steel cooking utensils, and other daily tools are stored by hanging. A simple style devoid of anything superfluous.

379

382

 | | Kenjiro Wada
Setagaya, Tokyo

As we conducted our interviews in different houses, from time to time people would ask us whose home we have visited beside theirs. Whenever we responded that we have been to Wada's home, it elicited a reaction. Wada's home, which the BEAMS staffs members all collectively describe as "the house with a particular, distinctive style," is a result of demanding the highest quality in everything from comfort to spatial beauty. From the furniture and lighting down to the tiles of the kitchen, everything has been meticulously selected, and each piece contributes to a unified whole. An unmatched home worthy of admiration.

What is the most important theme of your lifestyle?
An expansive, open space.

How do you like to spend your day off?
On sunny days, I like to relax on the roof balcony, my favorite place.

What is your theme or rule for interior design?
Be demanding down to every last detail, such as the walls, the tiles, the switch, and even the soap bar. Take your time examining everything closely until you find your favorite; never purchase anything in a hurry.

What is the most cherished item in your home?
I like vintage, well-used furniture with character. I love our Tapio Wirkkala table, which we searched for nearly a year and waited for it to come back in stock even though it was inconvenient for us to wait that long.

Do you have any collections or things you can't resist buying?
Traditional costumes from the Middle East, Asia, Africa, and so on. I am attracted to one-of-a-kind pieces, clothes and textiles with painstakingly detailed embroideries and decoration that are unthinkable to do in contemporary times. Ever since the earthquake and tsunami in 2011, I've been gravitating toward textiles rather than bowls that can easily break.

Do you have a favorite interior design brand or store?
Playmountain in Sendagaya; Swanky Systems in Minami-horie, Osaka.

Do you have any advice for people who have trouble keeping a tidy home?
Don't place things unnecessarily.

What kind of fashion style do you like?
Basics stylized in a fresh, innovative way.

Which fashion brands do you prefer when creating your own sense of style?
Scye; Copano; Yo's Yo.

How do you hone your sense of style?
Don't accept things as they are. Try to look at things from many different angles.

1. The tiles used for the kitchen walls were ordered from Heath Ceramics, a longstanding ceramics maker based in San Francisco. Tiles with engravings are mixed in to create a fun, eclectic canvas, while their subtly altering shades of color add further character. Heath Ceramics kitchenware are also sold through BEAMS, and we found several items in Wada's home as well.

2. The terrace, Wada's favorite place, is used for BBQs and outdoor parties on the weekends.

3. Stored inside the antique *mizuya tansu* kitchen chest from the Taisho era are an array of pottery purchased throughout Japan. Alongside pottery made in Yachimun, Okinawa, and the *Mashiko-yaki* from Tochigi prefecture, there is pottery from Kyushu prefecture, where Wada is from. With plenty of dishware for entertaining, it's no wonder they have so many guests.

4. The floor has been entirely redone in oak. A rope door-stopper at the side of the living room door. Along with the finest gems of design chairs placed around the living room, the fusion of folk crafts and mid-century modern invigorates the comfortable space.

388

🏠 | 👪 | Shuji Suzuki
Kamakura, Kanagawa

Suzuki's home is protected by *Yato*, a unique landscape structure of Kamakura City. In a land that he discovered as if he were drawn to it, Suzuki, with the help of a renowned carpenter in Kamakura, has built a home that incorporates myriad architectural techniques and the formal beauty of traditional Japan. His home is a place to savor the warmth of things made by hand while enjoying the view of the different seasons passing through the backyard. This space, into which Suzuki has poured his heart and passion, can be described as a living folk craft, where tradition and the modern meet.

What is the most important theme of your lifestyle?
I try to live thoughtfully, surrounded by good food and sake, as well as by handicrafts from around Japan and the world.

What is your theme or rule for interior design?
I position my furniture and everyday items so that I can always live surrounded by family memorabilia and beautiful, handcrafted items. I try to store away unnecessary things as much as possible. I also utilize the walls as much as possible for storage, so that I can secure space for living.

What is the most cherished item in your home?
Pottery, glassware, and baskets.

Do you have a favorite interior design brand or store?
Moyai Kogei.

Do you have any advice for people who have trouble keeping a tidy home?
If I think I might not use an item for a while, I try to let it go, even when it's hard.

What kind of fashion style do you like?
I like a style that is simple and has meaning (or a story). Design and detail are important, but so are color and material.

Which fashion brands do you prefer when creating your own sense of style?
This may count as part of BEAMS, but I like Fennica.

Are there any magazines, books, or people that inspire your interior design and fashion?
When it comes to handicrafts and culture, someone I look up to as a mentor is Keiichi Kuno, the owner of Moyai Kogei in Kamakura.

How do you hone your sense of style?
Get to know various local cultures by traveling through Japan and the world.

1. Suzuki took out a sheet of graph paper on which he had illustrated the layout of his home. He talks joyfully of how he found a land in Kamakura, ordered lumber in Hida Takayama in Gifu prefecture, and spent half a year building his home. The deep love he has for his home is evident in its every aspect.

2. The idyllic residential landscape and nature of Kamakura can be seen from the kitchen window. Kamakura, which is cool in the summer and warm in the winter, offers the most ideal climate.

3. Suzuki placed the stone paving in front of the entrance piece by piece with a friend. The exterior wall made of lumber has been treated with the most advanced coating material available to ensure longevity. "The home may seem old, but modern technique is used in various ways."

4. The second-floor mezzanine, accessible from the living room by a ladder, is where a collection of large bowls and pots are kept. The most elaborate feature of this home is the floor, which combines timbers of varying types and sizes. The technique, called *chosen bari*, was developed in the traditional homes in Korea; it is quite rare to use this technique today because it requires great amount of time and effort. The painstakingly constructed floor has the warmth that only things made by hand possess.

394

🏠 | 👪 | Yosuke Fujiki
Tama, Tokyo

The handmade nameplate is not the only reason this house overflows with love, even from the outside. As soon as we open the front door, a multitude of photos and paintings, seemingly stacked at random, comes into view. While the home preserves the stylishness of the building as it was originally built, the living room has been renovated to accommodate Fujiki's growing family. The open staircase leads to a booklover's heaven upstairs. Why are books, music, and art necessary in life? This home, with its impeccable taste, invites such discussions to take place.

What is the most important theme of your lifestyle?
If you are asking me what's most important, my answer is "love."

How do you like to spend your day off?
I do what I want to do in that particular moment.

What is your theme or rule for interior design?
It changes from day to day.

What is your favorite spot in your home and how do you like to spend time there?
It changes from day to day.

What is the most cherished item in your home?
A photo of my daughter three days after she was born, taken by a professional photographer.

Do you have any collections or things you can't resist buying?
I don't collect anything in particular, but I'm attracted by completely useless things.

Do you have a favorite interior design brand or store?
Interior décor created by my family.

Do you have any advice for people who have trouble keeping a tidy home?
Perhaps there is no need to tidy?

What kind of fashion style do you like?
I like the kind of style featured in the last scene of *Kids Return*, the Takeshi Kitano film.

Which fashion brands do you prefer when creating your own sense of style?
Colony Clothing.

Are there any magazines, books, or people that inspire your interior design and fashion?
Art exhibits.

What do you hope to purchase next?
Time to travel the whole world.

How do you hone your sense of style?
Live as your heart desires.

What is your personal mantra?
Time is love!

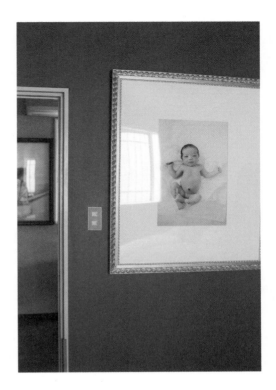

1. Books are displayed even on the stairs leading to the attic, which is not ordinarily used. Fujiki explains that the arrangement of things in his room changes according to his mood, transforming each day.

2. "I like handmade things, regardless of whether they're good or not," Fujiki says. An array of painting and drawing tools are scattered on top of the table with a handmade sign.

3. The curious mobile hanging from the ceiling is a book by Yasumasa Morimura. "I look at things as if they are alive."

4. A study filled with light at the top of the stairs. The corner of the study is Fujiki's workspace, where ideas for exhibits and projects for his gallery were born.

5. A true gallery employee, Fujiki has an impressive collection of art books from the world over, and the genres represented on his shelves are eclectic. The books are an excellent match for the succulents spotted everywhere around the room.

399

400

 Yo Shitara
Meguro, Tokyo

BEAMS' repertoire is not limited to fashion but encompasses music, interior design, and almost anything related to lifestyle. Where and how does Shitara, a CEO of such a brand, live? We let our curiosity guide us into his home, where we conducted this interview.

I understand you designed this home. Has interior design always been your strong suit?
I've always loved architecture and interior design. If it were up to me, I would have loved to work in a creative field as an architect or interior designer. However, even though I was always pretty good at sports and design, I was neither strikingly gifted nor did I have a special talent. That's why even now I still have both admiration and a complex toward artists like photographers, painters, and musicians. And yet it is precisely because I love so many different things that I'm able to select and work with the top artists. I've begun to think that this is another way of creating, so now I see the value in what I do and consider my job my calling. If I was better at designing or playing soccer, perhaps there would have been no BEAMS.

You said you are as interested in interior design as you are in fashion, but did these two fields always carry the same weight for you?
When you hear BEAMS you may think of an apparel company specializing in fashion, but we actually got our start as an "American life shop." When we launched as a tiny store (approximately 230 square feet) 38 years ago, we already had skateboard wheels and candle stands we purchased in the U.S. on our shelves; the concept of the store was based on the American collegiate lifestyle. These days, there are many so-called lifestyle shops that offer various ways to live and experience culture, but we have always endorsed a kind of lifestyle that includes furniture, miscellaneous accessories, and clothes. I like to think that fashion and interior design exist to enhance our lives for the better.

The homes of the BEAMS staff members we interviewed for this book have a lot of variety, but they also have many similarities. How do you define the BEAMS quality that they share?
People who want to work at BEAMS, even if their personality or taste is different, find the same kind of style and atmosphere comfortable. In other words, I think what they have in common is a kind of ease; they are not rigid or fixed. Rather than a meticulously structured coolness, BEAMS is about comfortable interiors where you can relax and hang out with friends. I think that kind of welcoming atmosphere exists in all of our stores as well. Instead of a cool and orderly product lineup, I prefer the excitement of discovering your own personal favorite among a pile of miscellaneous items, like you would do at a flea market. That's why you can find folk dishware, Scandinavian furniture, and American toys all in a room belonging to one BEAMS staffer.

Perhaps the reason why so many BEAMS staffer excel at mixing various things instead of unifying everything under a single taste is because Beams is curatorial— it's a "select

shop." I've even said in the past that "BEAMS is Tokyo blend." I value the unique aroma and depth of flavor that you get when you blend various things together. That's what's fun about select shops.

Speaking of select shops, BEAMS was a forerunner, wasn't it?
"Select shops" were not part of the lexicon back when BEAMS was founded 38 years ago. In reality, it's impossible for one person to buy all their clothes, food, and items for the home from just one brand. That's why I feel it's such a natural inclination to select things. I'm proud that I was able to shake up the industry in the sense that I was able to create the concept of the select shop itself. I think it changed the course of the generation in a small way. What makes me feel glad to have started BEAMS is when I'm able to be a part of the transitional period of a generation. This is something you only become aware of when you look back in time. We feel today that certain clothes, furniture, or cars are very '70s, but back then people were not aware of that. I feel so happy when I know that something that BEAMS or a BEAMS staff member introduced has caused a small change in the generation; I love being there when that happens and sharing it with people.

There's something very BEAMS about how the brand transmits an authentic lifestyle.
Many of BEAMS numerous labels started spontaneously. For example, one of our staff became pregnant but she couldn't find anything she wanted to wear so she made a maternity clothes label. Beams Boy was founded because we had so many female customers who preferred men's clothes, but they could not find them in the right size.

Rather than conducting marketing out in the world and figuring out what sells from a business strategy standpoint, many of our labels were born of the needs that arose in the everyday life and changes that our employees experienced. Perhaps that's the reason why we were able to survive for 38 years. The power of our staff is undeniable. When we open a store, even when I have a complete image in mind, I never tell them to create the store exactly the way I envision it. I only communicate the concept and the feeling that the store should have. Depending on how the staff digest those ideas, the end result can far exceed my imagination and reach 120% satisfaction. I think there's a chemical reaction that occurs when people relate to each other and exchange ideas.

Right now, authenticity is also important in the way we sell our products. Before, we made it a priority to communicate the intention of the creator: the singular vision of the designer, the history of the brand, and various other factoids about the product. Now, we go beyond that, putting emphasis on communicating how happy it makes you when you actually use the product—what kind of lifestyle you can attain and how fun it can be. Customers can see how our store staff have styled the clothes, talk to them, and hear their opinions on the products' efficacy. All of that connects to the joy of shopping in person rather than online.

Speaking further, I think what we're doing is to offer a dream that's attainable with a little bit of effort. No matter how wonderful the product, something that's prohibitively expensive isn't realistic. I feel more in balance when I can

sell what I actually wear and use on a daily basis rather than trying to sell a Mercedes while living in a tiny room. I want people to find our products aspirational; they should find them appealing even as it makes them wonder, "Would I be able to wear this? Is it a little bit expensive? Will this match the interior of my home?" When you reach a little higher than you normally would and attain that item, it often ends up enriching your life and turning into something invaluable.

You've seen, touched, and used so many different things. How do you go about selecting things today?
There are two patterns to the way I select things. First is to select masterpieces with history. For instance, I still keep and treasure my vogue collection from the '30s to the '70s. The second pattern is the antithesis of the first. I collect kitschy items that only exist for an ephemeral moment, things that make you chuckle. For example, one of my favorite items these days is a toy whistle that makes a sound of a dog barking. I love things like that and can't help but purchase them.

I don't care too much about price. In my home I display Scandinavian glassware of superior quality that I found abroad, but among them is a flower vase that I purchased for about 300 yen at a flea market. Same thing for the photos mounted on the wall. Among the original monochrome prints I have a picture that I cut out from a book and framed myself. But no one who visits my home can tell which one is the cheaper item. I put things I like on an equal plane, and it makes me smile when a connoisseur comes over and heaps praise on the cheaper item. I don't think only

having expensive and superior things is necessarily stylish. Whether it's fashion, interior design, or human relationships, I think imperfection is important. Imperfections, I believe, leads to interesting conversations.

What would you advise to someone who hopes to attain a stylish life?

How about starting out by purchasing a chair? You'll have to think it over long and hard before you finally make your purchase. But once you buy a chair that speaks to you and put it in your home, that alone should change the feeling inside your home dramatically. Then, start selecting accessories and other furniture that go well with the chair and expand from there.

When figuring out what you really like, your root is also important. There is something I always ask the new employees of BEAMS: "What is the first thing you purchased with your own money?" Records, vintage denim, hair accessories, a small basket—the answer depends on the person. But the answer tells me a lot about that person's history. Our taste is our root and it's written in our DNA. For me, it's American. Of course, my tastes are swayed by short-term trends, but something that I've always loved is American style. That's the style I still find the most comfortable, so my room always looks like a throwback to the original BEAMS store.

What we like is the starting point for everything, then?

What you like is very important. Many of our BEAMS staff were long-time fans of the store. Of course, it's a job so there's tough times too, but they can get through them because they like the brand. I've always said that "Hard work can never beat obsession." You become obsessed because you like something, and things you do because of an obsession is powerful. Your passion brings other like-minded people together and that's how a commune is formed. Going forward, I would like for BEAMS to become a community brand. Not a company but a community; that's what I'm striving towards. I want us to be a brand that is a community that employees, the creators, and customers would want to join. As I always say, what we are aspiring toward is a happy life solution community.

Hard work can never beat obsession. That's a lifestyle philosophy, Shitara-style.

I believe it. And that belief always brings people together. Right now, what's more important to me than physical things are events, meaning life itself. And events naturally connect people. At the end of the day, I think clothes and furniture exist to connect us with family and friends. They are all tools for communication. Of course, wearing what you like and displaying what you like in your room is a form of self-expression, but how other people view and feel about those things can start a conversation. You feel good using certain things but what's also important is how that contributes to how you interact with others. It makes us the happiest to live among things and people we like the most.

What we offer as a company now has never changed from before: We strive to be happy.

That sentiment is reflected in the name of the company, too.

There are three meanings to the word "beam". First is light beam, to cast a beam of light on the various things we have yet to discover. The second is beam as in pillar. The beams are piled together to support our customers and our employees. Lastly, just as we say, "beaming face," we define beam as an adjective, meaning a smile that shines like the sun. I think all of the staff members' home introduced in this book radiate with such bright, shining happiness. It's not a catalogue of products; it shows people living joyfully in a room with a comforting, positive outlook. And it fills me with joy that the people represented here are wearing and using BEAMS product in their daily lives.

1. A refined Japanese style room with Ryukyu tatami floors. Displayed on the *tokonoma* alcove and blending seamlessly into its surroundings with the Japanese scroll is a Swedish Dala horse.

2. A basement room dedicated to Shitara's hobbies and interests. The room comes equipped with a professional bar counter and sound equipment, making it a perfect place to watch movies and karaoke with friends. The furniture and decorative items tend to have an Eastern bent, as they are items that Shitara has brought home from various Asian countries.

3. Chairs have been among Shitara's longtime favorite items, and he has amassed an astonishing 64 chairs over

the years! From cheap finds to designer items, the chairs come from myriad countries and generations. It has always been Shitara's dream to design the interior of each room around the particular style of a chair.

4. A modern space made of white walls and stone tiled floors. Here Shitara displays vintage items he found in various parts around Asia from China and Thailand to Vietnam. Left: View from the entrance. Hanging on the walls are Shitara's favorite platinum prints, collection of Scandinavian glassware, and paintings. The theme of Shitara's home: "A room with the ease of a gentle breeze, where you can almost hear the sound of the waves."